Praise for

WHY DIDN'T WE RIOT?

"A powerful lesson in history and truth...Through a combination of poignant memoir and social and cultural analysis, Bailey tackles a range of hot topics as well as his own prior complacency."

—*KIRKUS REVIEWS* (STARRED REVIEW)

"An essential and powerful call for action."

—*LIBRARY JOURNAL* (STARRED REVIEW)

"Impassioned...a bracing and timely survey of why Black Americans are 'sick and tired of being sick and tired.'"

—*PUBLISHERS WEEKLY*

"[Bailey's essays] are incisive as they confront the realities of systemic racism in America...essential reading."

—*FOREWORD REVIEWS*

"As a Black man who has persevered to assert the truth and uphold integrity in his work, Bailey offers an unflinching perspective about the ongoing dialogue about racism and racial justice in America...While Trump is now out of office, this book is as relevant as ever."

—*SEATTLE BOOK REVIEW*

"Bailey's voice is worth listening to…a shrewd call-out of the undeniable racism emboldened by Trump's presidency."

—SHELF AWARENESS

"Singular voices have arisen that are able to separate the wheat from the chaff to openly speak the truth about the continuous violence perpetrated upon Black people and the rising inequality in Trump's America. Issac J. Bailey is one such voice…Bailey splendidly creates a milieu where empathy can take root and blossom within readers of all backgrounds."

—NEW YORK JOURNAL OF BOOKS

"In Issac J. Bailey's book, James Baldwin meets James Bond—that is, Bailey performs a kind of racial spy mission, bringing back intelligence from deep in Trumpland about the kind of thinking that continues to have disastrous consequences for our country. *Why Didn't We Riot?* is a very important book."

—CLIFFORD THOMPSON, AUTHOR OF *WHAT IT IS: RACE, FAMILY, AND ONE THINKING BLACK MAN'S BLUES*

"This is such a timely book, delivered into our hands at precisely the moment when we are reckoning with the cruel legacies of racism and inequality in a manner we never have before. A searing, honest, and essential read for anyone who wishes to know how we got here, and how we might escape."

—TOPE FOLARIN, AUTHOR OF *A PARTICULAR KIND OF BLACK MAN*

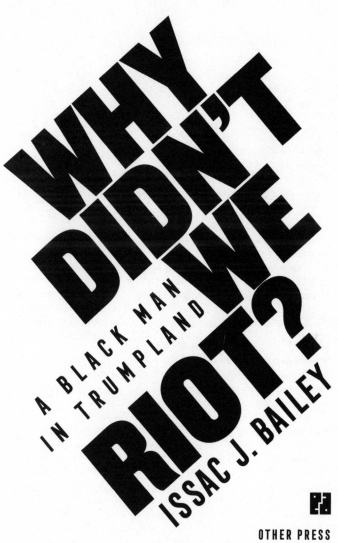

WHY DIDN'T DID'NT WE RIOT?

A BLACK MAN IN TRUMPLAND

ISSAC J. BAILEY

OTHER PRESS
NEW YORK

First softcover edition 2022
ISBN 978-1-63542-221-4

Production editor: Yvonne E. Cárdenas
Text designer: Julie Fry
This book was set in Swift and Avant Garde
by Alpha Design & Composition of Pittsfield, NH

10 9 8 7 6 5 4 3 2 1

Library of Congress Cataloging-in-Publication Data
Names: Bailey, Issac J., author.
Title: Why didn't we riot? : A black man in Trumpland / Issac J. Bailey.
Description: New York : Other Press, [2020]
Identifiers: LCCN 2020008891 (print) | LCCN 2020008892 (ebook) |
    ISBN 9781635420289 (hardcover) | ISBN 9781635420296 (ebook)
Subjects: LCSH: Racism—United States—History—21st century. | United
    States—Race relations—History—21st century. | African Americans—Social
    conditions—21st century. | Discrimination in law enforcement—United
    States. | Police brutality—United States. | African Americans—Crimes
    against. | African Americans in mass media. | African Americans—Politics
    and government—21st century. | Trump, Donald, 1946–
Classification: LCC E185.615.B263 2020 (print) | LCC E185.615 (ebook) |
    DDC 305.800973—dc23
LC record available at https://lccn.loc.gov/2020008891
LC ebook record available at https://lccn.loc.gov/2020008892

Preface

IN A SCENE from the 1992 Denzel Washington–directed movie *Antwone Fisher*, the central character shows up on the doorstep of his childhood foster home and is greeted by a woman who had spent years sexually abusing him when he was young.

"Come here, baby," she greets him.

"Don't touch me," he snaps.

He is no longer a little boy, but rather a man matured by the U.S. Navy.

"I'd like to speak to Mrs. Tate," he tells his tormentor, referring to the foster mother who had spent years treating him like a disposable diaper and "beat me to dust" until he ran away at the age of fourteen and got into trouble before finding his way into the military.

Fisher was placed with the Tates, a deeply religious couple, when he was two years old. His father had been killed before he was born. His teenage mother gave birth to him while she was in jail.

"Oh nigga, hug my neck!" Mrs. Tate says with a smile while trying to embrace him, as though she were a long-lost friend, not an evil that had nearly destroyed Fisher.

He doesn't hug her neck or any part of her, doesn't smile, doesn't pretend to want anything to do with her. He doesn't need an apology she doesn't think to offer. He neither wants nor needs her approval. The scars are still too fresh, too deep, all those years later.

"You couldn't destroy me," he says, defiance dripping from every syllable he speaks. "I'm still standing. I'm still strong! And I always will be."

I'm Antwone Fisher to white America's Mrs. Tate. I don't want it to be that way. But I don't know how to be otherwise. The scars are too deep, too fresh. I knew we were in trouble when I couldn't find a way to not be angry, because I had never been angry before, not in a sustained way. If a black man like me was having trouble corralling his anger, I knew it meant that anger among black people had to have risen to biblical proportions and could ignite given the right spark. I just didn't know that spark would be eight minutes and forty-six seconds of a video of a white cop slowly, defiantly snuffing the life out of a black man on the concrete in broad daylight in front of numerous onlookers.

As I type these words in June 2020, I get that the Confederate flag came down after the massacre in Charleston. I appreciate that cities, counties, and police departments have begun rethinking their use-of-force policies, that police unions are being pressured to allow reform or get out of the way. Symbols of white supremacy are under attack—monuments, memorials, *Gone with the Wind*—in a way I had never seen in my lifetime. Demonstrators throughout the world called George Floyd's name in solidarity with black Americans. New York repealed a law that had kept police discipline records private. Lady Antebellum became "Lady A."

Protesters chopped off the head of a monument built in honor of Robert E. Lee, the man who led the Confederate army. They threw a statue of Christopher Columbus into a lake. Clemson University trustees voted to remove the name of slavery champion John C. Calhoun from its Honors College. The mayor of Boston declared racism a health emergency and dedicated $3 million in funds to deal with it. NASCAR—yes, NASCAR!—banned the Confederate flag from all its properties and events. Even *The Bachelor* has named its first black lead.

Still, I'm jaded. That's why I'm having a hard time processing how to feel after years of banging my head against a brick wall and finally seeing cracks emerge. I'm not yet convinced white people are willing to do what it would take to enact the changes we need, even after the most sustained and widespread protests of my lifetime. I fully expect that even after all we've seen, all the harm Trump has done on the issue of race, and so many other things, that he is more likely to garner 60 percent of the white vote in November than 50 percent. I fully expect that he will win the white vote at every economic level the way he did in 2016. I fully expect that if Trump finds a way to get a second term, it will be because white America decided that white supremacy and racism aren't deal breakers—even in 2020.

The immediate changes made in the wake of the Floyd protests were positive. But they were low-hanging fruit. White supremacy and anti-black racism have to be pulled up by the roots in order for long-lasting reform to take hold. If that doesn't happen, if there is no real racial reckoning, history will repeat itself. The past has made that clear. When I was a student at Davidson College in North Carolina in the early 1990s, I sat in my dorm watching on CNN scenes from the L.A. riots after the Rodney King verdict. Not too long after I finished teaching a couple of journalism courses at Davidson during the spring 2020 semester, Floyd was murdered by police in Minnesota.

White supremacy meant a race-based chattel slavery would be further entrenched after black people helped white colonists defeat the British. It meant Reconstruction, during which black people made significant steps forward even though they were only recently freed from slavery, was followed by Redemption and the rise of the Ku Klux Klan and a century of lynchings. Black excellence along "Black Wall Street" in Tulsa was met by mobs of white vigilantes and their friends in the military and police who murdered hundreds of black people and left thousands homeless. Black veterans were treated worse than German POWs during World War II. White supremacy convinced white parents and school officials to be defiant in the face of a 1954 Supreme Court that supposedly killed Jim Crow—then convinced white voters to follow the era of the nation's first black president with the election of a man whose rise to political heights was powered by the open use of bigotry and racism.

I interviewed the famed civil rights attorney and civil rights crusader Bryan Stevenson after his organization opened the nation's first memorial dedicated to the nearly five thousand people known to have been lynched throughout much of the twentieth century. He spoke about how the Holocaust Museum motivates every visitor to say "never again."

We haven't done that for the legacy of slavery in this country.

"We haven't created spaces that present the history of racial inequality in this country in a way that motivates people to say never again," he said. "Because we haven't said never again, people say things that are ignorant about enslaved people being responsible for their slavery or being lynched, or segregation being something that black people wanted. I think that mindset has just not been disrupted by the truth of what our history is. I do believe the truth can make us free. Understanding what has happened, despite its brutality, is key to us creating a better future."

Neither have we fully grappled with the trauma inflicted upon those wearing dark skin in a supposedly free country.

"I don't think we understand what trauma does; I don't think we appreciate how we have institutionalized a lot of trauma by the way we have been indifferent to basic human needs," Stevenson told me. "From enslavement, where 50 percent of all enslaved people were separated from their spouse or their family members, that's traumatic. Lynching, to have people of color hanged and brutalized and tortured while others cheer is absolutely traumatizing. To have to learn how to exist in a society where your humanity is constantly denied and demeaned by segregation can be incredibly traumatizing and injurious. And even now, to live in a country where if you are black or brown and can be presumed dangerous and guilty just because of your color. And to have to navigate around other people's presumption of your dangerousness, when you are not dangerous, it's exhausting."

I'm exhausted. Most black people I know are exhausted.

While I want to be encouraged by what we saw after the murder of George Floyd, I can't—not yet. Pulling down monuments and furling the flag of traitors that should have never been flown on public property—or demanding that police officers kill only when absolutely necessary, as a last resort and not because they were afraid or angry—might get us closer to zero, but it won't guarantee true racial equality. Too much damage has been done. The wounds are still too fresh. I'll know white America is serious about long-lasting change when they begin to punish politicians who use white supremacy and white fear as political weapons and tools. The first Tuesday in November will begin telling the tale.

Introduction: Trumpland

IN NOVEMBER OF 2019, I was invited to participate in a panel discussion at Davidson College about the 2020 election cycle. It featured John Kasich, former governor of Ohio, 2016 presidential candidate, and favorite of MSNBC's *Morning Joe*. Bill Kristol, a longtime conservative and one of the nation's highest-profile Never Trumpers, was also on the panel, which was moderated by Davidson political science professor Susan Roberts. Kristol was teaching a course on ethics at Davidson that semester. I was teaching a course on journalistic empathy and ethics, and another about Donald Trump, race, and the American news media.

Kasich was the featured guest and spoke for about a half hour, then we commenced with the moderated discussion. His well-crafted image as a compassionate conservative from a purple state known for its bevy of down-home, hardscrabble, white working-class residents was likely why a student group chose him to visit a college known for its mostly liberal student body. The students chose me to round out the perspectives that would be represented on the panel. But before the panel, we dined at the college president's house. It was there, about a month before the House of Representatives would vote to impeach Trump, that I encountered the unexpected.

As I ate a dinner roll, I couldn't help but overhear Kasich waxing poetic about how great things were going in the United States. He'd focus on the same theme during his public talk, about the importance of being optimistic, about how "you don't have to move a mountain to make a difference."

It was a great time to be alive, to be an American, he proclaimed. All the anguish people were expressing in the Trump era was overdone. Checks and balances all but guaranteed that President Trump could not cause much damage, not even on the contested issue of immigration, he explained to those sitting at our table, which included a handful of students and Professor Roberts. There's lots of talk about negative things occurring in the Trump era, but little proof, he said.

Before I sat down for that dinner, I had vowed to not say much. I wanted the students to interact with Kasich, knowing I'd be able to do so later. I got through most of the dinner having said little, other than a few niceties and an introduction. That changed when Kasich kept saying there were no real problems, that even the much-discussed issue of immigration turned out to not be problematic. He talked about the low jobless rate. He noted the stock market's rise—and that the forecasts suggesting it would tank had been woefully wrong. He asked everyone around the table if they had any real problems and said it sure didn't seem like it, that he was doing great. He recounted how the deportation rate under Trump was not significantly different from what the country experienced during many of the Obama years, the kind of out-of-context fact I have long warned my students against using.

"Well, the *legal* immigration rate has dropped by seventy percent since last year," I quickly chimed in, expecting him to acknowledge that maybe he had inadvertently papered over a more complex reality in his quest to remind us to be grateful to be American. Instead, he told me I was absolutely wrong, that such a big drop wasn't possible.

The courts did not allow that, he told me. And there was no "Muslim ban" because we have constitutional checks and balances, remember? Everyone needs to stop exaggerating problems, he said.

We went back and forth for a few minutes. I'm a lifelong stutterer. The stutter worsened when I was a nine-year-old boy trying to process what it meant that my hero big brother had committed murder and was taken away to prison. The stutter followed me into adulthood, and during some passionate discussions, it presents unique challenges. But during the back-and-forth with Kasich, I refused to let my stutter stop me. Before we headed to the Duke Family Performance Hall, where the panel would be held, he pulled out his cell phone. He relayed what I said to the person on the other end of the line, asking if it was true.

"Yes," the person told him.

I then handed Kasich my phone and showed him an article from the *New York Times*. "Immigration Population Growth in the U.S. Slows to a Trickle," its headline read.

"The United States population gained immigrants at the slowest pace in a decade last year, according to an analysis of new census data, a notable slowdown that experts said was quite likely linked to a more restrictive approach by the Trump administration," the story by *Times* reporter Sabrina Tavernise said.

The net increase of foreign-born people in the United States fell by 70 percent from the previous year, to a total of about 200,000 people in 2018. During the Trump era, the world watched as the president repeatedly demonized immigrants and enacted policies that treated them as less than human. It wasn't just the kids in cages; it was the kids stolen from their parents to deter families fleeing violence elsewhere from seeking refuge here. It was his disgusting, racist rhetoric, his attempt to implement a Muslim ban, his decision to close America's doors to refugees and make a mockery of the poem inscribed at the base of the Statue of Liberty. While Trump supporters have claimed they are only against illegal immigration, few of them raised a stink about the effect Trump's bigotry had on the rate of even legal immigration, let alone the slowdown at our southern border, where Trump suggested it would be okay to shoot potential immigrants and asylum seekers who threw rocks at U.S. military and security personnel.

How could Kasich have read or seen headlines about all of that, and more, and not realize what was happening to everyday, vulnerable Americans and potential Americans? I don't mean to pick on Kasich. As I told him, he was on my short list of potential presidential candidates I was considering in 2016. His insistence that we not take for granted the privileges we've been afforded in this country is a good thing. We should not overlook our blessings or the progress this country has made and continues making. Our exchange was telling because Kasich is known as one of the most plugged-in politicians in the nation, someone who knows how to properly balance his Washington-insider status with an ability to remain in touch with the everyday man.

He had led a state Trump won fairly easily. He was one of the first Republican governors to accept the Medicaid expansion through the Affordable Care Act when other Republican governors—like Nikki Haley in my native South Carolina—decided to deny money their most desperate residents were in need of, all to remain in the good graces of the far right. And yet, he didn't know about the well-documented damage Trump's rhetoric and policies have inflicted upon communities of color.

Immigration was only one such issue. During the panel discussion, he claimed he had "solved the race thing" while governor of Ohio. Never mind that Ohio was home to twelve-year-old Tamir Rice, who had been gunned down by a police officer within two seconds of that cop's exiting the patrol car upon arrival at the park where Rice was playing with a toy gun—in a state in which leaders like Kasich made it legal to openly carry real guns.

He sounded a lot like a host of national political pundits and analysts who were quick to scold people of color for not being grateful enough and complaining about Trump too much. It has grated on my nerves for the past few years. Constitutional checks and balances may have shielded the most vulnerable among us from Trump's worst excesses, but Trump, through policy and rhetoric, has been able to inflict an enormous amount of damage anyway. That was true even though the jobless rate was low and the stock market was high at the time. (I wonder if his tune has since changed given that the 2020 pandemic unleashed by coronavirus has further revealed decades-deep inequalities that have made communities of color more susceptible to the horrors of Covid-19.) Telling us to focus solely on those things—and ignore what we are experiencing daily in places like these—is akin to telling the battered woman to ignore all the weekends her husband beats her and just be grateful for the times he brings her flowers and says he loves her.

I couldn't be quiet at that dinner table for the same reason I had to write this book, as a kind of corrective to such banal commentary. I grew tired of people ignoring us or telling us to shut the hell up and just take it, or that we weren't "resisting" in the right way. I grew tired of pundits, analysts, and researchers parachuting in and declaring they had figured out how we should handle a time like this, even though they clearly knew little about what we faced, and seemed to not really try to understand.

I grew tired because I know all that those like me have done to become and remain friends with people who repeatedly disappoint us, particularly on the issue of race. There have been days I've visited restaurants and received poor service from white waitresses who likely assumed I wouldn't tip well—and gave them a large tip anyway, to counterbalance the stereotype of black people as bad tippers. I know some white waitresses assume that about black people because they've told me. I've patronized white-owned businesses that didn't even have the decency to turn off Sean Hannity or Rush Limbaugh while serving me, and I would feel guilty if I "punished" them for their conservative beliefs and leanings by avoiding those businesses. But the pundits who lament white guilt know nothing about that form of everyday black guilt in Trumpland.

Trumpland includes places throughout the United States where white people overwhelmingly support Trump in spite of—or maybe because of—his open bigotry and racism. They are places where black people have for decades been forced to swallow racist bullshit in order to respect the wishes and wants and feelings of racists, as well as those who excuse and apologize for the racists. They are places largely but not only in the South, like

Horry County, South Carolina, a place where even though the population is getting whiter, Trump fans lament the infinitesimal effects of illegal immigration. These places have become Trumpland, not only because Trump became president, but because so many of our white friends from elsewhere, particularly liberals and moderates, professors and professional pundits among them, demanded that black people here swallow hard once again, to not be too angry, to not say that the Trump supporters we know much better than they do are racist, as though protecting them from that label is more important for the health of this country than helping us achieve racial equality.

In Trumpland, up is down. Those on the receiving end of Trump's racism are told it is we who must change in order to keep the peace and the illusion of civility and unity intact. In Trumpland, black people are told once again to go quietly to the back of the bus.

I don't speak for all black people in Trumpland. But what I've experienced is not an anomaly among black people in red and purple states. We love this place as much as, or more than, anyone. That's why we felt betrayed by our white neighbors, friends, and colleagues who helped make Trump president in 2016 and why we've been frustrated by supposed allies since then who seem more concerned with the wants, needs, and beliefs of those who harmed us.

That's why you need to know what it's really like here, from someone with a lifetime of firsthand experience. This book is for Harvard professors who misuse the term *identity politics* in a way that suggests black people in Trumpland should just shut up and take it. It is for Never Trumpers who spend more time speaking out against those of us angry with the state of things than they do trying to rid the White House of Trump and his bigotry. It's for the white liberal and white moderate whom Martin Luther King Jr. alluded to all those years ago in his "Letter from a Birmingham Jail," those who prioritize peace and calm over justice and equality.

Black people everywhere face the struggle that is race and racism and are angry in the age of Trump, given that White America in 2016 decided to make a man like Trump president. But in Trumpland, it is different. It is harder to escape. That's why this book is for those who have either forgotten or have never known what life can be like for a black person who has to navigate a region in which the blood of their enslaved ancestors still fertilizes the soil; the flag of their enslavers flies freely just about everywhere; and statues and monuments and memorials built in honor of those who raped and beat and lynched our great aunts, uncles, grandmothers, and grandfathers greet us at the schoolhouse and the courthouse and in the public square.

Here, we are sick and tired of being sick and tired. This book explains why.

White Comfort More Important than Black Life

AS A WHITE COP TOLD ME he had regretted not shooting a black man in the head, I nodded along, trying to better understand his point of view, to empathize with him just a little more. I didn't scream. I didn't feel an urge to punch him in the mouth or shake him. I just sat there, nodding along as though I was listening to the tall tales of a friend I hadn't seen in years but had long admired.

He told me how he had initiated what he believed would be a routine traffic stop somewhere near Charlotte, North Carolina. He told me how after approaching the car and noticing a few things that made him suspicious, he began thinking of ways of stalling until backup arrived to help him; how he made small talk with the two young black men in the car to keep things on an even keel. I forgot what, specifically, made him suspicious or why he stopped the car, but I'm sure he said it had nothing to do with the skin color the men in the car were wearing. No matter, because his instincts were right.

Before his backup arrived and as he was making small talk, the man in the passenger seat was suddenly trying to pull a rifle from underneath his seat between his legs. That's when this white cop pounced on that black man, with one hand struggling to prevent the man from lifting the rifle, the other unholstering his own gun, which he promptly pointed at the man's head. If everything he told me was true, it would have been a justified shooting. He would have had to go through the mandated procedure every cop who shoots someone goes through. He'd be taken off the streets and relegated to desk duty until an internal investigation cleared him, which is the most common result of most police shootings, even with less clear circumstances.

Instead of pulling the trigger, he reholstered his gun and began fighting the man for control of the rifle. The fight seemed to last a lifetime as his backup made its way to the scene, that cop told me.

"I got my ass kicked," he said.

He also secured the arrest of a young man who had a long criminal record and bad intentions that night. Though he got his ass kicked, he was able to hold on long enough for help to arrive. Though he got his ass kicked, he had no life-threatening injuries, and neither did the young black man. It was proof—absolute proof—that even during moments in which a police officer might be "justified" in shooting a suspect in the head, it wasn't as necessary as many police officers and their defenders claim. It was proof—absolute proof—that sometimes if a police officer is willing to get his ass kicked, he can save a life and prevent yet another incident that will potentially create distrust between police and the communities they patrol most frequently. That distrust, once rooted in, makes it exceedingly difficult for the community to embrace the police presence many of them need. It makes it less likely that community members in distress would be willing to call 911—because they fear the cops more than the criminal down the street—and more likely they will take matters into their own hands, which fuels cycles of violence as much as poverty.

He could have rethought everything he had been taught about how to make an arrest under seemingly impossible circumstances. He could have told his fellow officers that maybe the shoot first, ask questions later to keep yourself safe mentality was outdated—and just plain wrong in more situations than they had considered. He could have told them that bravery is required when you are granted a uniform and a badge and trained and paid and given the power to ruin—or end—lives, the kind of bravery that says a suspect's life is as important as your own. He could have reminded them that, as far as being killed on the job, being a police officer is not among the most dangerous professions, despite the persistent myth much of the public clings to. Loggers, roofers, steel-workers, sales workers, and truck drivers are killed on the job at higher rates than police officers. There has been no safer time in U.S. history to be a police officer. As former *New York Times* reporter Blake Fleetwood noted, in some large cities like Chicago, the average citizen faced a murder risk three times higher than the average cop. The black man being stopped by police late at night on the side of the road has as much, or more, to fear than the cop who initiated the stop.

Instead of considering those realities, the white cop who told me his story harbored and nursed regrets for *not* shooting a black man in the head. His fellow officers made sure he wouldn't forget how wrong he was—for *not* shooting a black man in the head. His colleagues didn't praise his bravery or quick thinking. They said he had unnecessarily put himself in danger. They said he had unnecessarily put the public in danger. "You got lucky," they said.

The chances for a promotion that white cop had been wanting suddenly evaporated. He felt isolated, his relationships with fellow officers grew strained. He was not commended. No medal was affixed to his chest in a public ceremony for having saved a life. He was scorned by fellow officers—for *not* shooting a black man in the head.

That fateful traffic stop happened only a few weeks after he had returned to patrol after he was cleared in a shooting during a different incident. He reholstered his gun because a quiet voice told him it would look bad if he shot another young black man. It was that voice, maybe borne of guilt, that saved that black man's life, not an altruistic act by a benevolent white cop. Or maybe it was the public pressure—from relentless activists who refused to be silent in the face of layers upon layers of racial injustices in the criminal justice system—that saved that black man's life, because their unrelenting voices made that white cop think twice before pulling that trigger again.

And yet, what he learned from having saved a life... was that he should not have done so, that it would have been better to have put a bullet in another young black man's head. Because that's what he was taught at the academy. Because that's what police trainers write best-selling books about and get paid to argue on CNN in prime time. While it's easy to slam Fox News for hiring Mark Fuhrman as an "expert" on race and police brutality despite (or because of) his infamous role in the O. J. Simpson saga, CNN paid "law enforcement analyst" Harry Houck to say black people are prone to criminality and that the real victims are cops.

The message sent to cops time and time again is that the public will be okay with whatever they do, especially in Trumpland. The comfort level of cops is more important than black life, and that's why a cop's right to shoot a young black man in the head to avoid getting his ass kicked, or worse, must never be challenged, must forever be sacrosanct, no matter the evidence that it is less necessary to keep the public safe than cops have been trained to believe it is.

What I learned from my reaction to hearing his story is that for too long, I had not been among those loud, unrelenting voices demanding change. Mine hadn't been one of the ones that likely saved that young black man's life that night. I learned that I had not done enough to remind police officers, and others granted an enormous amount of power, that we expect them to be better, to not value their own lives above others. I learned that I had spent so much time trying to empathize with them and understand the supposedly daily threats they face, in an effort to build bridges I believed others had been burning, and too little time holding them to account. I learned that there are plenty of black people in Trumpland like me. We swallow our anger. We deny our fears. We hope against hope that our continuing efforts to reach out will be reciprocated. We do this even when we are the ones being killed or maimed or threatened by men and women in uniform we pay to protect us.

That's why I understand Brandt Jean's emotionally powerful gesture in a Texas courtroom. Jean was the eighteen-year-old brother of Botham Jean, a young black man who was gunned down by white police officer Amber Guyger. She claimed to have mistaken his apartment for her own and, startled to see a strange young black man there, shot him dead. In a surprising twist, the police department didn't declare her actions justified after an internal review. Instead, she was charged with murder, a rare occurrence for a white police officer shooting and killing a black man, even when they are off duty, as Guyger was when she made her way into Botham Jean's apartment. More surprising still, a diverse jury found her guilty of murder—the rarest of outcomes in such situations—and sentenced her to ten years in prison, even after the defense invoked the kind of stand-your-ground law that has helped countless white people get away with killing black people. Despite what some have claimed, a ten-year prison sentence is significant. It's true that her sentence is shorter than those given to many black people, especially those who have committed murder. But the answer isn't to call for longer sentences for people like Guyger, but shorter sentences for everyone else. Those who know anything about America's prisons know why. Prison isn't a place I'd wish on my worst enemy. It is dehumanizing. Ten minutes, let alone ten years, inside those walls can be hell.

In those circumstances, Brandt Jean took to the witness stand in that Texas courtroom and gave a victim impact statement that reverberated around the country.

"I love you," he told the white cop who murdered his black brother.

"I don't want harm to come to you," he told the white cop who murdered his black brother.

"I want to give you a hug," he said before the judge granted him the right to embrace the white cop who murdered his black brother.

"I forgive you," he said.

White America wept at the sight of such grace. "One day, I hope to have as much faith as Brandt Jean," a white conservative writer I know quickly tweeted.

Black America was moved, too, but in a different way, and struggled to reconcile its deep faith—the very one that convinced Brandt Jean to forgive the white cop who murdered his black brother—and the broader implications of such a powerful act. I was with Black America. By then, I was no longer prioritizing the feelings and perspective of white people and white cops.

We aren't against forgiveness, we just know that throughout American history, that's what black people have been required to do, and do so willingly, only to see White America pocket those acts of grace and hardly ever return the favor. After slavery—slavery!—we did not seek revenge, we only sought equality. After a century of lynching and convict leasing and Jim Crow, we did not take up arms to do to White America what White America had done to us. After we helped defeat Hitler in a military that still wanted to segregate us and treated German prisoners of war better than black American men in uniform, we did not revolt, or when we did, our spasms of grief resulted in the burning of our own communities, not white ones. We picked up placards and put on our marching shoes to demand equal justice before the law. When White America spat in our faces, told us we were too ugly and too unworthy to be treated with fairness, we kept marching, our goal only equality, not racial domination.

In 2015, when a young white supremacist prayed with us in one of our oldest, most revered churches, then killed nine of us in a Bible study slaughter, we forgave—only to see our white Christian brothers and sisters pocket that act of grace, congratulate themselves for finally furling a Confederate flag that should have never flown at our statehouse, and thanked us by making a bigoted Donald

Trump president. That's what Black America was thinking as it watched White America tell us how moved they were by Brandt Jean. That's why, though we understand why Brandt Jean did what he did, we were not in the mood to sing hosannas with White America.

Because we knew—and still know—that had the roles been reversed, White America would not have wanted to sing hosannas with us. Because we knew—and still know—that had the roles been reversed, there would have been no forgiveness, no hugs. Because we knew—and still know—that even though White America claimed it was deeply affected by Brandt Jean's act, had Botham Jean been the killer and Amber Guyger the victim, she would have been valorized, no matter how many mistakes she had made. Because cops are presumed innocent, black men guilty, no matter the circumstances. That's why police officers felt comfortable leaking Botham Jean's supposed history of smoking marijuana to suggest he was "no angel." We know that had Botham Jean been the killer, he would have either received the death penalty or life in prison. We know that had he killed her, his name would be constantly evoked to push harsher laws that would inevitably hurt black people more than any other racial group. It would have been used by those getting rich off a false "war on cops" narrative that threatens to curtail the tame criminal justice reform efforts that have received bipartisan support in recent years.

In the minds of too many white people—liberal and conservative, Christian and non-Christian, cop and civilian—the natural state of things is for black people to be forever-forgiving victims, no matter the circumstances. That's what makes White America most comfortable. And for too many in White America, nothing matters more than that, especially not black lives.

The Uncomfortable Truth about Black Men and Violence

VIOLENCE HAS A WAY OF CLARIFYING THINGS.

Liam Neeson, the actor best known for the *Taken* movie franchise and his "I have a particular set of skills" line, admitted that he once dreamed of murdering a random black man after a friend told him she had been raped by an unidentified black man.

"I went up and down areas with a cosh [a bludgeon], hoping I'd be approached by somebody—I'm ashamed to say that," he told the newspaper the *Independent* in February of 2019 while promoting a movie in which he portrays an angry father seeking revenge for the death of his son. "And I did it for maybe a week, hoping some 'black bastard' would come out of a pub and have a go at me about something, you know? So that I could...kill him."

He went on to express remorse, saying he was ashamed and surprised he had ever thought such a thing and received help to better understand why he had, and to ask for forgiveness. His explanation did not sit well with critics who still deemed him racist for forty-year-old thoughts.

"You are a representative of racial terror," a *New York Times* columnist tweeted to Neeson.

I guess I am, too. Because violence has a way of clarifying things, often in disturbing ways.

IN THE HOURS AFTER LEARNING that my would-be sister-in-law was murdered in a drive-by shooting, I could focus on little else than thinking of ways to put the black dudes who killed her behind bars as quickly as possible. I was scared. I was angry.

Usually when I tell this story, I mention the bloody footprint that greeted me at the apartment door where the shooting occurred and my desperate need to prevent what I knew would be another round of violence in my small, rural hometown if the shooters weren't caught. The part I don't much like admitting aloud was the blood-lust coursing through my veins, the kind Neeson was referring to as he detailed how he picked up a crowbar and walked into black neighborhoods hoping to instigate a fight with a black man—any black man—because his friend had been assaulted.

I wanted the young black dudes who killed Kim—an incident I'm reminded of every time I look into the eyes of my niece—to not just be caught, but suffer. Truth be told, though I was afraid Kim's death would spark another round of violence, I would not have shed a tear had those young men been felled by a bullet, too. I didn't care any-thing about their humanity, their backstory, or what factors—maybe witnessing domestic violence, watching drug sales and violence in their neighborhoods, suffering from abject poverty since birth—could have contributed to their decision to pick up the guns they used to kill Kim. They were nothing to me.

They had caused great harm; I wanted great harm to be inflicted upon them. Because violence has a way of clarifying things, often in disturbing ways. It's the kind of thinking I knew my brother Jordan, the real target of the bullets that killed Kim, was engaging in, even though he spoke very few words.

Moral concerns and constitutional principles, and even a belief in redemption for those among us who have com-mitted the worst acts, can become secondary in the imme-diate aftermath of violence. Police officers feel it when they get word that a fellow officer has been killed. Gang members feel it when a fellow gang member has been shot. Fathers feel it when their daughters have been harmed.

It's why politicians know the story of a single crime victim is as powerful as a thousand inspiring tales of for-merly violent men who have become positive contributors to society. It's why even the staunchest criminal justice reform advocates make a clear distinction between non-violent and violent offenders. The former are redeemable, the latter not. It matters not that the line between those who act upon the kinds of dark things Neeson was think-ing and those who don't is uncomfortably thin.

Violence perpetrated upon someone you know, some-one you love, can momentarily make you insane, or despondently amoral, if you're lucky. That's why when some family members of the nine people massacred by Dylann Roof in a Charleston, South Carolina, church for-gave Roof, it was powerful and moving. It was surprising because we expected anger and bitterness to reign during those moments, which tells me that though many people expressed disgust about Neeson's comments, they under-stand them, too.

I even understand why Neeson's rage was aimed at "black bastards," because I've felt that, too.

Neeson only felt that way after confirming with his friend that her attacker was black. I didn't ask if Kim's murderers were black. I assumed they were. This is where I want to lie and tell you my assumption was simply logical. My youngest brother is black. Most of his allies and rivals in the violent illegal drug game in our area were black. I've long known that most violent crime is intraracial.

While I knew all of that, my assumption came from a deeper, darker place. For years, racist stereotypes about young black men had lingered in my brain. I'm a black man. I have eight black brothers. My father was black. My stepfather—a man who stepped in to help my mother take care of a single-wide trailer full of kids after she left my father—is black. I know that the totality of black men who commit murder on an annual basis doesn't even add up to a half of one percent of all black men in this coun-try. I know my dark skin hasn't made me violent.

And yet, none of that prevented me from thinking ugly thoughts about fellow black men. When I've admitted this to friends and confidantes, they insist upon drawing a bright line between me and Leeson. That white actor is the real racist because his ugly thoughts could have led to an innocent black life being violently taken, they told me. That's true. But mine could have led to the same place. A black man as informed as I am about the racial injustices inherent in our criminal justice system should know better than most why it's important to not allow black men to be demonized. Such demonization makes it easier for the public to be okay with black men being abused by the police—or by each other when they are shipped off to prison and remain behind bars for decades. Neeson's acute racist thoughts, triggered by a violent act, could have led to something much worse. Everyday racist thoughts about black men like mine have; they are the foundation and fuel of mass incarceration. And I know I'm not alone, no matter how much I've learned about the urgent need for radical racial justice. Because violence has a way of clarifying things, in awful ways.

My experiences and knowledge could not inoculate me against fearing and loathing my own dark skin. It never crossed my mind that someone other than a young black man could have carried out the drive-by shooting that murdered Kim. If such thoughts could invade my soul, they could invade Neeson's and the thousands of white people who celebrated and gawked at innocent black men and black women being lynched for much of the twentieth century—because they wanted some black bastard, any black bastard, to pay the way Neeson wanted—and the millions of white people who don't want anyone to know such thoughts have invaded their minds, too.

It's easier to tell the incomplete story, the part that leaves out what else I've experienced in Trumpland as a black man. I've sat in all-black churches hearing black people demonize young black men, even on Father's Day. I've sat in all-black settings, in small gatherings in homes and restaurants, hearing black people demonize young black men who have done awful things, or *might* do awful things. I've heard black people say things about young black men that would give white supremacists wet dreams. In their telling, many young black men are just the random black bastards of Neeson's imagination. Because violence has a way of clarifying things, often in ugly ways. It feeds and waters nasty stereotypes like little else, even in the minds of those targeted by the stereotypes.

In many ways, the reality I faced as a black boy and young black man nearly guaranteed I'd succumb to such awful thoughts. I grew up helplessly watching my father's black fists land on my mother's flesh. When I was a nine-year-old black boy, I watched my oldest, hero black brother be marched away in handcuffs and shackles after he stabbed a man to death. A black friend from high school is blind to this day because of a bullet that lodged in his brain. A young black dude I helped mentor in college was killed by a police officer—as he was killing another police officer. Those images have taken up more space in my mind than those of watching my second- and third-oldest brothers become huge successes, and other brothers and first cousins do the same. It's why so many black people helped build our mass incarceration infra-structure on the backs of black men—and, increasingly, black women—and are sometimes ambivalent about help-ing those who are trying to destroy it. It wasn't just Joe Biden and that 1994 crime bill or Hillary Clinton and her "super-predator" comments.

Because violence has a way of clarifying things, often in disturbing ways.

Violence and dark skin have been so thoroughly linked because of what I've seen and experienced—and because of the images the local TV news, major media outlets, and Hollywood keep feeding me—that I've had to struggle against my own mind. In some particularly tough moments, I sometimes lose that battle. I've some-times given in. It's why I felt almost no concern about my own brother's safety in the aftermath of Kim's shoot-ing. In that dark moment, I felt nothing for him. I'm as ashamed to admit that as Neeson is ashamed of what he almost did.

Because violence has a way of clarifying things—in disturbing ways.

The Truth about Black People and the American Dream

I'M NOT PROOF THAT AMERICA IS GREAT.

I'm not proof that anything is possible.

I'm not proof of American exceptionalism and meritocracy.

I'm proof of the resilience of black people in a country which long deemed dark skin a sin.

Here is the truth: on most days, I still feel like the helpless little six-year-old boy crouching in the corner of the kitchen in my house watching my father beat my mother and not knowing what the hell to do. Those psychic scars haven't healed, let alone disappeared, nor could they ever be forgotten. They haunt me in ways known and not. There is no escape from their reach. I didn't know then that my father pounding his fists into my mother's flesh wasn't simply an individual act by a disturbed man, but a culmination of events in a society that made my father—born into a South in which the criminal justice system re-enslaved black men for the use of private corporations—a pariah since he was an embryo in my grandmother's womb. I hated my father for what he did to my mother. I should have spent more time despising the society that molded him.

I teach at a top liberal arts college. I was paid to spend a year at Harvard University. I've been published by and featured in several major news outlets—print, online, and broadcast. That doesn't mean I've pulled myself up by my bootstraps. None of it means I am a "credit" to my race or "don't seem black," as I've been told too many times by white people in Trumpland. They mistakenly believe that's a compliment, though it's just another way to hide their demonization of black people with a smile on their chins and a pat on our backs.

Let me tell you what I am: a broken man with a broken past who fears he's inevitably headed toward a broken future. I don't want your pity, though, don't need you to believe I'm a forever victim forever licking his wounds and cursing his pain. I'm not.

I know how to handle challenges, overcome obstacles. I've spent a lifetime perfecting the craft. That's what being black in America requires of you. I'm not the world's only broken person. I'm not special. I simply want you to understand a hard truth about what it means for a black man in the South, deep in the heart of Trumpland, to have achieved the American dream, to know that it is often accompanied by nightmares.

That's why I no longer tell my story the way Dr. Ben Carson tells his, pretending it's all or mostly a result of hard work and good decision-making. Because it's not true, not the full truth. Because I know that too many white people have grown fat on sweet lies about success- ful black people, so much that their appetite for racial equality has been satiated. They use my presence, and the presence of others like me, either to fight policy and soci- etal changes that can lead to further progress or to feel comfortable ignoring the subject altogether. For too long, I've allowed them to. I no longer will.

In February 2013, Carson became a darling of the right during the Obama era when he took to task the sig- nature legislation of the nation's first black president— the Patient Protection and Affordable Care Act—during what was supposed to be an apolitical speech on the National Day of Prayer. The right suddenly had a new, high-powered black mascot and eagerly used his story to downplay concerns about inequality. Dogged individual effort was all that was needed to beat the greatest odds, just as Carson taught us, they said. Talk of racism was just excuse-making and evidence of a victimhood mindset, they proudly proclaimed. It wasn't happenstance that he became the only black cabinet member of a presidential administration headed by an open racist and bigot like Trump. Before he became a hard-right conservative hero, Carson was an icon in most black households, with black mamas and black daddies telling their little black boys and little black girls that we should grow up to be like Carson, the personification of black excellence.

Carson would later try to clarify his thinking, saying he was in favor of safety net programs for those who need them, but only those who need them. His comments in May 2014 on ABC's *The View* are representative of how Carson's story is now perceived, particularly by those who believe racial disparities are a product of black laziness and ineptitude:

> When you rob someone of their incentive to go out there and improve themselves, you are not doing them any favors. When you take somebody and pat them on the head and say, "There, there, you poor little thing...Let me give you housing subsidies, let me give you free health care because you can't do that." What would be much more empowering is to use our intellect and our resources to give those people a way up and out.

The irony of Carson rising to fame in the American right by dumping on the nation's first black president is that the American right initially loved Obama (or at least didn't despise him) when he talked about his story of overcoming discrimination and a poverty-stricken one-parent household, the kind of story conservatives love to hear successful black people tell. Obama declared that his story was only possible in America. Conservatives especially loved it when Obama said this during his national debut at the 2004 Democratic National Convention: "The pundits like to slice and dice our country into red states and blue states—red states for Republicans, blue states for Democrats. But I've got news for them, too. We worship an awesome God in the blue states, and we don't like federal agents poking around in our libraries in the red states. We coach Little League in the blue states and, yes, we've got some gay friends in the red states."

It's the kind of sentiment that made everyone feel good and perpetuated the myth of America, even if Obama didn't intend this. But the American right hated Obama any time he mentioned anything other than the rosy parts of our history, as he did by refusing to paper over the complexity of the unrest in Ferguson after the killing of Michael Brown by a white police officer and decades of police misconduct.

"The frustrations that we've seen are not just about a particular incident: They have deep roots in many communities of color who have a sense that our laws are not always being enforced uniformly or fairly," Obama said in televised comments as protesters and police clashed in Ferguson. "That may not be true everywhere and it's certainly not true for the vast majority of law enforcement officials, but that's an impression that folks have and it's not just made up—it's rooted in realities that have existed in this country for a long time."

Obama was speaking a truth many white conservatives (and a good number of white liberals) don't much want to hear. They wanted him to simply condemn the black protesters. They wanted Obama to put "his people" in their place, not explain black people's frustration and angst. When he didn't, they accused him of being divisive and the cause of racial violence. The white reaction to Obama's words, which included a call for peace and calm, respect for authority and the arrest of those committing violence, made it clear that to be black and remain in the good graces of white conservatives (and a good number of white liberals), a black man must never critique the United States of America in ways white people don't approve—especially if that critique includes an unapologetic examination of the harm white supremacy and white racism have caused and continue to cause. Carson seems to understand that as well, which is why he, Obama, and I have—or had—something in common.

When I spoke before largely white audiences, I'd detail my tough upbringing. I'd paint verbal Picassos about growing up in a literal tin can of a green-and-white single-wide mobile home—tin roof, tin sides—in the heart of the Old South. I was forced into a segregated school system and saw the few white classmates of my elementary years sent to a school eight miles away to keep them from having to go to high school with unintelligent, violent black bastards like me, I'd recount. Then I'd talk about how I watched white police officers wrap cold steel around my hero older brother's wrists and waist and ankles at my father's funeral to take him back to prison. The final masterstroke would be mentioning my lifelong struggle with a severe stutter that resulted in constant ridicule and name-calling when I was young and denied job opportunities when I became a man. I didn't have to say that no matter those struggles, I was able to rise above them anyway. My presence on those stages said it for me.

I thought I could convince them to not give up on young black people who were still in the middle of the struggle I had faced. I thought I was convincing them that those young black people needed second and sometimes third chances—as I had; thought I was breaking through, building racial reconciliation bridges. I desperately wanted to believe that by sharing the challenges I faced, it would melt hearts, reopen minds. Instead, too often the response was: "You made it. Why can't *they*?" The *they* was always a reference to young black dudes who were running the streets or failing in school or headed to jail or prison. The story I told about my journey too often hardened rather than softened hearts. Which is why today I tell a very different version—a less self-aggrandizing one, which includes the truth of my relentless stubbornness in the pursuit of excellence, but without the self-made man bullshit.

My story includes being ashamed when Mama sent me to the grocery store with a handful of food stamps. We needed the help. I knew we needed the help. I was ashamed because people like Carson told people like me we should be ashamed, as a way to stave off potential government dependency, even though government helped stave off starvation in my family. Ironic, isn't it, that Mitt Romney and Donald Trump could receive "small" loans from their multimillionaire parents, and billionaire hedge fund managers can proudly take advantage of absurdly out-of-whack tax laws, but a black teenage boy growing up in a small town a short drive from where the Civil War began felt shamed because his family needed food stamps. Not to mention the poor black women I've known over the years whose shame for receiving any government assistance convinced them it was wiser to take on two or three low-wage jobs at once, even though it meant their young kids had little supervision throughout most of the day and would later be killed on the mean streets at night.

Large rectangular blocks of government cheese and bags of white beans and boxes of powdered milk and King Vitamin cereal helped sustain us. I received unearned breaks from teachers who could have failed me during the moments I didn't work hard. Pell grants and invites to government-sponsored programs for gifted students and silent prayers from strangers were among the million reasons why I ended up a professor, not a prisoner. I received handups *and* handouts. It wasn't just my wit and hard work and discipline that made me who I am.

I'm not a self-made man.

But my story is more than that. I'm broken because of what I've had to face in a country that was founded upon white supremacy, yet struggles to admit that simple truth. I still speak with a stutter that's linked to watching my hero big brother be taken off to prison when I was just a nine-year-old boy. I still suffer from PTSD that grew out of my early childhood struggles, a mental disorder that showed up as extremely violent daydreams about harming my wife and kids, or later as violent daydreams about a small dog I rescued from a shelter but had to return within nine days. I called her JoJo.

She was about nine months old. She was less than a foot tall, as long as my arm and weighing no more than a normal-sized toddler. Her fur was brown and black. She had whiskers like a cat and strands of hair hanging from her chin like an elderly woman who had long stopped grooming herself. Her eyes were soft. She liked to cling to me and never wanted to be more than a couple dozen feet away, even while running around at the park. But after I adopted her, the PTSD-related violent images I had been treated for began invading my mind again. I thought they might lead me to hurt JoJo, though all she had shown me was love. I was too broken to know how to accept her unconditional affection.

Not only that, I've struggled, along with the rest of my family, for several months watching Mama remain in a physical state just above vegetative after she endured a stroke and more hardships than I have, struggled because I desperately want to talk to her again, seek her counsel, and because I'm afraid I'm headed for the same fate. Because I've learned that the body never forgets, that significant and persistent early trauma lingers in the body for decades, long after you've overcome the great odds you are supposed to be proud of having beaten. That's one of the reasons black life expectancy is less than white life expectancy, why black people in their fifties and sixties are more prone to succumbing to chronic diseases than similarly situated white people, and maybe why I developed an autoimmune disease in my forties.

Our accomplishments despite all of that are evidence of a legacy of black strength and black resilience that stretch back millennia. America didn't make us; we are remaking it. More than 200,000 of us took up arms during the Civil War to save this country from itself. Black journalists like Ida B. Wells chronicled the lies and myths that led to thousands of black men and women being strung up and burned alive by white domestic terrorists. Black men like John Lewis endured life-threatening beatings at the hands of white supremacists to persuade America to live up to its supposed ideals and refused to become bitter about it. Obama became president in a country that had declared during its creation that men like him weren't fully human. And, yes, even Carson is a part of that legacy, having overcome so much to become so brilliant, even if he believes too much in the myth of America.

Our bodies, our scars—psychic, emotional, physical— are evidence of a sickness that has been with us since before this country's founding and, like a virus, morphs and transforms, constantly seeking new hosts to remain alive no matter whom it maims or kills. I, a black man from the South, am proof of white supremacy's persistence *and* limitations. It means I'm a carrier of white supremacy in the way I'm a carrier of chronic inflammatory demyelinating polyneuropathy, or CIDP, the autoimmune disease I was diagnosed with in 2013.

My white blood cells began attacking my nerves and shutting down major muscle groups, my body turning against itself for reasons science still can't fully explain.

The aggressive treatment designed to stop the disease's march nearly killed me. Though there's no test I can take to confirm it, the constant stress I was exposed to since I was a little boy could have led to a lifetime of inflammation that was changing my body's internal wiring every day even though I didn't know it, culminating in CIDP. Occasional stress can be healthy, teaching the body how to cope. Persistent stress puts the body in a near-constant state of emergency, making it difficult for the body to moderate itself, rendering people like me less capable of discerning the line between real and imagined threats. Maybe that's also why a subconscious part of me viewed cute, harmless JoJo as a potential threat and triggered my PTSD. The worst part, though, is knowing all of this—that "toxic stress" kills and ruins lives—but never being able to say it definitively, because the science isn't that finely tuned yet. Racism kills. Literally.

When CIDP descended upon me, there were days I neither could walk nor had enough strength to fold a large towel. Since those dark days, I've made enormous progress. I'm in remission. I'm back to jogging six miles a day. I'm healthier than many people who never experienced anything like CIDP. But my body isn't like it was before. Scars remain, as does CIDP. I can still feel the subtle disruptions and tinglings beneath my skin that were with me long before my diagnosis that I hardly paid attention to because they caused no immediate or detectable pain.

What CIDP did to me, white supremacy has done to the United States. Its causes are myriad, though largely mysterious and mystifying. The damage it leaves in its wake is often subtle, though pernicious. Sometimes its presence can't be ignored when it announces itself in violent spasms. It's why no discussion about white supremacy can be complete without examining the roles we all play, not just those played by Trump supporters or even avowed white supremacists. It's not just about those carrying tiki torches or committing massacres in black churches or synagogues. White supremacy flows through this country's DNA the way CIDP flows through my veins.

It's not happenstance that there has never been racial equality in America, a country which coupled race-based chattel slavery with its demand for liberty and justice. That makes the black story unique in ways I wish it wasn't. We don't know what it feels like to just be American in a country that from the beginning hated and despised us for being black, and now hates and despises us for refusing to relinquish that blackness. And yet, here we are, still rising. Though they enslaved us, we didn't give up. Though they lynched us, we didn't give in. Though they kill us on video in broad daylight and hide behind shiny badges to absolve themselves of all responsibility, we refuse to back down.

I didn't have to take the Adverse Childhood Experiences test or study trauma's effects on the developing child's brain, as I did at Harvard University for a year, to know that truth. I can feel it in my bones. I can't *not* feel it. I can hear it subtly coursing through my veins. It colors everything I think and feel. That's the part of the

American story many don't want to hear, that we "over-comers" have wounds that won't heal, that can only be managed, that we must reconcile ourselves to. That's not a cry for help; it's a scream for recognition, not for those of us who have trod the stony road, but for those still making their way up the rough side of the mountain.

The Banality of White Supremacy
in Trumpland

The function, the very serious function of racism, is distraction.
It keeps you from doing your work. It keeps you explaining,
over and over again, your reason for being. Somebody says you
have no language, so you spend twenty years proving that you do.
Somebody says your head isn't shaped properly, so you have
scientists working on the fact that it is. Someone says you have
no art, so you dredge that up. Somebody says you have no kingdoms,
so you dredge that up. None of that is necessary.

    There will always be one more thing.

— TONI MORRISON

A FEW WEEKS BEFORE Dylann Roof massacred nine black people in a historically black church in Charleston, a gaggle of white police officers a two-hour drive away treated an apartment in Myrtle Beach as though it was a house in Fallujah during the height of the Iraq War. The young black man they shot is expected to be paralyzed for the rest of his life. Roof was sent to death row in a federal prison in Terre Haute, Indiana, for his deeds. Those police officers were praised for theirs. No one told me to mince my words when writing about Roof. I could be as nasty as I wanted to be while describing my feelings about him. But in discussing the police, I was scolded, warned not to be too harsh.

In Trumpland, black people mustn't criticize cops, no matter how many times or in how many ways they hurt us. It's unseemly. It's un-American. U.S. Attorney General Bill Barr spoke for many when he essentially told black people to not be too uppity.

"I think today, American people have to focus on something else, which is the sacrifice and the service that is given by our law enforcement officers," Barr said in late 2019 during a speech while presenting the attorney general's Award for Distinguished Service in Policing. "And they have to start showing, more than they do, the respect and support that law enforcement deserves—and if communities don't give that support and respect, they might find themselves without the police protection they need."

In other words, if we don't let cops disrespect us, brutalize us—and occasionally kill us—without making a fuss about it, we don't deserve the police protection our tax dollars make possible. It's less important for black people to be protected from criminals than it is for cops to be uncritically supported, even when they abuse us, help prosecutors secure convictions based on falsehoods, plant guns and drugs on our brothers, or throw our sisters around like rag dolls. The banality of white supremacy—white people turning a blind eye to all forms of white supremacy not draped in a Klan robe or proudly announcing itself—reigns where I live.

Former South Carolina governor Nikki Haley unintentionally summed it up well while speaking with right-wing talk show host Glenn Beck about the aftermath of the Roof shooting. "Here is this guy that comes out with this manifesto holding the Confederate flag and had just hijacked everything people thought of it. We don't have hateful people in South Carolina. There's always the small minority that's always going to be there," she said. "People saw [the Confederate flag] as service and sacrifice and heritage...but once he did that, there was no way to overcome it...And we had a really tough few weeks of debate, but *we didn't have riots*, we had vigils. We didn't have protests, we had hugs. The people of South Carolina stepped up and showed the world what grace looks like."

To white supremacy, grace looks like black people being praised for swallowing our anger or labeled radical if we refuse. If we suck in our tears, stiffen our backs, and stoically and silently endure, they will furl a flag that should have never flown. They pocket our acts of grace and never have to do the hard work of confronting and uprooting centuries of racial injustice and disparity. They brag about the interracial hugs we share after a white supremacist massacre in a black church. They say nothing when officers shoot black men for selling a drug that's making white people in other states rich.

Make no mistake, that kind of thinking isn't the sole domain of Trump supporters and white conservatives. White liberals here often demand it, too, including a friend who told me I was turning an ally into an enemy for speaking forcefully about yet another white police officer shooting yet another black man. He votes for Democrats. He preaches racial equality. He was more angered by my refusal to accept the death of an unarmed black man at the hands of police than by the killing itself. It can be exhausting being black in this place. That's why sometimes we've whispered when we should have roared. We've acquiesced when we should have said hell no.

That's why maybe black people should have rioted after what Roof did and what those cops did, because it seems to be the only way to get white people to pay attention. We should have made clear just how angry we are, how angry we've long been. We should have cared less about white comfort, more about equality. But fighting racism nonstop in a place that uses our tax dollars to honor the men who raped our ancestors can feel futile. Having to fight for racial equality against white neighbors and friends who want to look the other way frustrates like little else. Listening to supposed allies explain it away wears you down. We wear the mask, sometimes too well.

That's why you've likely never heard of Julian Betton. Haley has never spoken his name. He was the young black man in Myrtle Beach police officers paralyzed for life. Two months before Roof shot up Emanuel A.M.E. Church, Betton supposedly sold two small quantities of marijuana to a confidential informant of the area's Drug Enforcement Unit. The DEU decided to send five heavily armed officers to break through the front door of Betton's apartment where they unleashed a barrage of bullets, at least nine of which hit Betton. They said Betton shot first, that they entered the apartment after clearly identifying themselves.

One officer told investigators this, according to a court ruling that allowed Betton to continue suing one of the officers: "I pulled the screen door open and announced in a loud voice 'police, search warrant.' The rest of the team had also made their way onto the porch and Agent Guess approached the front door. As Guess approached the wood door he knocked and announced again 'police, search warrant.' Upon no answer at the door force was utilized to gain entry into the apartment."

Another officer said this: "Agent Belue pulled open the screen/storm door to expose the primary entrance door. Another agent knocked and all agents, including myself, began to yell 'Police Search Warrant' prior to making entry."

Yet another officer said this: "At this point, I approached the front door, in which we had already knocked and announced 'police search warrant' with no response, and hit it with a ram. I yelled 'police search warrant' as the door opened up."

Myrtle Beach police officer David Belue, a member of the DEU, said he "distinctly remember[ed]" Betton firing his weapon.

They were all lying. We know they lied because an independent investigation determined it. We know because video from cameras Betton had installed after being robbed a couple of weeks earlier said so and because Betton's neighbor told investigators he saw the cops enter without knocking or saying anything. We know they lied because the forensic evidence investigators tested proved that not only had Betton not fired at the officers first, he had not fired his gun at all—even though he had been startled in his own house by strange men.

Betton was coming out of the bathroom in his apartment when he heard his door being "kicked or rammed open." He didn't hear anyone yell "police," didn't even hear the dozens of gunshots as they rang out.

"I said what the fuck to myself and reached for my gun," Betton told investigators. "And I woke up in the hospital being told I had a shootout with the police."

I had an intense argument with my editor in the middle of the newsroom after she tried to convince me to soften the words in a column I was writing about the shooting. She didn't want me to demean the police officers. She knew, as I knew, how our mostly white readership would respond. She knew, as I knew, that local police officers and their supporters would be more upset with me for telling the truth than they were that a phalanx of officers had lied about paralyzing a young black man for no good reason. I also knew there would be few, if any, repercussions for those officers from public officials—black or white—or from the public at large. Because I knew that in the minds of many people in Trumpland, black men losing their lives — or the ability to walk — after being shot by police was an acceptable trade-off if that's what it took to make white people feel safe and comfortable.

And that's what happened. Not long after my column was published, I heard from police officers, angry and disappointed, including a black woman police chief who scolded me. I heard the same from readers, irate that I had been "allowed" to say such things in print. The silence from other readers and members of the public who knew how disgustingly wrong the police were, was deafening. That happens frequently here, too frequently. We just let it go.

I later spoke to the local prosecutor, Jimmy Richardson, who had called that initial press conference praising the officers. On the record, he would only say he was going on what he had known at the time. I spoke with elected officials, black and white. Not one of them would say what they would do to ensure that such a shooting wouldn't happen again. They remained silent even though most defendants had already settled the case for nearly three million dollars. (Myrtle Beach later settled for an additional $8.5 million, claiming it was advised to do so by its insurance carrier.) I didn't hear from a single police officer in the area who thought it was a bad shooting, on or off the record. Never mind that we came to learn that no-knock raids had become commonplace and were repeatedly creating unnecessarily dangerous situations in residential settings.

During a deposition, the DEU commander was asked why none of the officers involved in the Betton raid had been disciplined. Because, he said, the officers "didn't do anything wrong."

Had black people in Trumpland decided to riot, or protested too loudly and "uncivilly," now *that* would have been wrong.

Riot conjures up images of "mobs" or "gangs" of black people stalking the streets with baseball bats staring down police in military gear and throwing Molotov cocktails. I'm not talking about that. I'm talking about a communal scream. I'm talking about a public declaration of black anger, the kind that scares those in power, scares white people, scares not a few well-off, comfortable black people. I'm talking about asserting our right, our moral duty, to not sit quietly, to no longer substitute calm for justice. We should have not allowed the police to go back to policing as usual without a reckoning. We should have demanded independent oversight of such incidents that isn't led by law enforcement officials. We should have said we would not relent until those officers were stripped of their badges and batons.

As Dr. King told us, a riot "is the language of the unheard." That's why so many are quick to pat black people on the head when our blood has been spilled, because that's easy, requires no sacrifice. It's a way for white people and black people to keep in place what historians who study the antebellum South sometimes refer to as the "Magnolia" and "Sable" curtains. During a time in which white people beat and raped and "sold" black people, white people believed black people saw themselves as beloved members of the white family and appreciated the guidance of their wiser, more moral white masters. That lie could only be sustained with the cooperation of black people, who went along with the ruse mostly to fend off white fears about slave rebellions.

"Whites felt safe, and refrained from state violence, as long as they could maintain a Magnolia Curtain, their shared assumption that slaves *would not* revolt because they knew they were loved as an extended black family," wrote David Robertson in *Denmark Vesey: The Buried Story of America's Largest Slave Rebellion and the Man Who Led It*. Vesey was one of the early members of Emanuel A.M.E., the church where Roof committed his massacre. That church sits on Calhoun Street in Charleston, named after one of the country's most prolific and effective slavery proponents and a short walk from a three-story-tall monument in that man's honor. Yes. We've built towering monuments to honor the enslavers instead of the enslaved. "Blacks found security, and avoided physical retribution, by playing their role of a people who *could not* revolt, whose mature emotions were secretly hidden from harm behind a Sable Curtain of pretended childish incomprehension or simple docility."

That "Bless your heart," "Jesus loves you" kind of white supremacy remains an unspoken rule in Trumpland. A white reader once proudly informed me that when she was growing up, her family loved—just loved!—a black woman who helped raise the white kids in the household. Yes, she said, of course they casually called that black woman *nigger* and made her sit in the kitchen to eat and paid her pennies on the dollar while that black woman's kids were neglected because that black woman had to spend so much time raising those white kids. That's just the way things were, the white reader told me. Besides, *nigger* was just a word, a descriptor. It wasn't like they strung her up on the Spanish-moss-draped oak or whipped her like a slave when her work wasn't up to par. To that white reader of mine, that proved their fondness for the black woman. The job her noble, white Evangelical Christian family *gave* that poor black woman helped that black woman's family make ends meet, even if barely. In their minds, they had gifted that black woman the occasional hug, granting her the glorious, if only momentary, touch of their white skin. Why wouldn't that black woman have been grateful? the white reader asked. She couldn't imagine that that black woman had simply chosen to keep quiet about all the times and all the ways in which that white family had treated her like a nigger, when they used the word and when they didn't.

I'm sure that black woman took it, stoically and proudly. I'm sure of this because black women on both sides of my family took it stoically and proudly when they had to work for white families under such circumstances. Had she shown anger—rioted in any way—she would have lost that job and the few dollars she was earning and would have been putting her life, and those of her family, at risk from white anger that often became white violence against those wearing dark skin.

White people have been rioting against black people since before the founding of the country, calling it "proper" and "natural" and "God-ordained" even as they insisted black people should not riot, too. Throughout our history, when white people rioted, they killed scores of black people, burned black businesses, overturned elections in which black people had emerged as the victors, and purposefully targeted black people who had found a way to become wealthy and educated despite the long tentacles of Jim Crow. White people never did those things because they were on the wrong side of racial disparities, because they never were. Still, as Oprah Winfrey said, they had a "quiet riot" because the verdict in the O. J. Simpson trial didn't go as they hoped, rioting because a lone rich black man had beaten a murder charge. They had reason to be angry that a double-murderer could walk free, but not to take it out on the black people around them. They've also rioted to maintain a "justice" system that routinely destroys black lives and undermines black families. They created Blue Lives Matter in response to Black Lives Matter. They don't care that Julian Betton is paralyzed or that the cops who shot him are walking free and being paid a salary funded by black taxpayer dollars.

They rioted after the tenure of the nation's first black president by placing a man in the White House who openly espoused racist views. Their safety has always been paramount, even when their safety was not being threatened. They've long reserved the right to priori-tize their own comfort, even when they only feel unsafe because of racist stereotypes traipsing freely through their own damn brains. So they lie to themselves and force black people in Trumpland to play along.

It's time for black people to stop playing along. It's time to tear down the Magnolia and Sable curtains, time to declare, once and forever, that black people refuse to go back to the back of the bus.

The Christian Knights
of the Ku Klux Klan

DONALD TRUMP'S RISE TO THE PRESIDENCY exposed an ugly truth, that there has never been a period in America's history during which white Christians unequivocally rejected racism. White Christians have not, en masse and without contradiction, made it an absolute priority to rid the country of racism, never said in one loud, unwavering voice that racism would be a deal breaker in a political partnership, or any other kind of partnership, even if they had to put other priorities on hold.

It's the primary reason white supremacy has yet to be fully uprooted, despite the racial progress the United States has made since the darkest days of the antebellum era. White supremacy can't survive in this country without Christianity. It's the only reason Trump could repeatedly do and say so many openly racist and bigoted things, because he's had the undying support of a historic percentage of white Evangelical Christians, even as Pew noted that nearly 90 percent of black Christians disapprove of him. They are the reason he is president. They are the reason he had any shot at being reelected. They are the only ones who had the power and influence to force him to change course. Instead, he forced them to reveal their faith-based hypocrisy.

I say this as a man who was raised as a Christian long before I understood what the word meant. I say this as a man who still prays but struggles to square the harm done in the name of the faith with the enormous good it has inspired so many to commit to doing. I say this as a man—a black man—who isn't sure he should still call himself Christian, particularly if the American version of Christianity can elevate a man like Trump to the most powerful office on earth.

"Has racism ever been truly incompatible with Christianity, as practiced in America? Rarely, I'd say. People have, unfortunately, found a way to keep those two things together," said Greg Snyder, a religion professor and colleague of mine at Davidson College.

Another colleague, W. Trent Foley, also in the religion department, made a similar point. "To my mind, the answer would be a fairly resounding no," Foley said when I asked if Christianity has ever been incompatible with racism. "In his 1969 book *Black Theology and Black Power*, theologian James Cone suggests that, historically speaking, there have been almost no antiracist white Christians in America—none certainly who were willing to make the ultimate Christ-like sacrifice on behalf of their black brothers and sisters in Christ—except for the abolitionist John Brown.

"There are perhaps some exceptions. In the nineteenth century, during the Second Great Awakening, there were some white revivalist preachers, most notably Theodore Dwight Weld, who preached that to be born again meant that, as a new being in Christ, one had to devote one's entire energy to the abolition of slavery," Foley continued. "Such revivalism helped, I suspect, to provide an impetus toward abolition movements in the north. Also, some denominations, especially Quakers, would boast that they also were against slavery and racism. But, clearly, to be anti-slavery is not to be anti-racist and I suspect that a lot of pro-abolition northern Protestants probably also had some fairly paternalistic and patronizing views of African-Americans—whether enslaved or free. Many of the Protestants, like Lincoln, might have thought their repatriation to Africa a good thing. So, I would judge that most white abolitionist Christians were still fairly racist."

I was born and raised and live in the Carolinas, the heart of the Bible Belt. Here, two things are prominent: Christian churches on every block, and monuments honoring those who fought to make black people permanent slaves.

Just a few miles from Davidson College is a multistory monument dedicated to "Our Confederate Soldiers." The dates of the Civil War, 1861–1865, and a cannon are chiseled into its sides, as is a Confederate flag. A stoic-looking soldier holding a rifle stands atop.

"Though men deserve, they may not win success," a dedication reads. "The brave will honor the brave, vanquished none the less."

It is protected by a black iron gate and a warning that anyone trying to vandalize it will be caught on camera and prosecuted. It stands in front of a large red-brick church with white columns welcoming guests at the front door and topped with a large green steeple. The congregation is predominately white. A white member told me she was torn about the monument's presence. She's been reluctant to make too much of a stink "because it was a sensitive subject," though she knows it makes it less likely that black people would take seriously the church's claim to be open to all.

Such statues, monuments, and memorials, as well as highways and schools named for the Confederacy, can be found in many states. Stacker, a data-analysis website, relying upon data gathered by the Southern Poverty Law Center, says twenty-nine states have at least one such monument, while twenty-one have none. North Carolina has 170; South Carolina 194. Only Georgia, Texas, and Virginia have more. They can be found on statehouses and in capitol buildings. I spotted a few outside of courthouses while reporting on cases involving poor, black defendants. They are seemingly everywhere.

The most direct link between white Christianity and white supremacy came in the form of a group that called itself the Christian Knights of the Ku Klux Klan, an offshoot of the most lethal terror group in U.S. history, which was still active in the Carolinas while I was growing up. When the Klan was at its apex, it committed atrocities that would make ISIS fighters blush, including burning black men and women alive in the public square as hundreds, sometimes thousands of white Christians looked on before passing around body parts cut from the lynched as souvenirs. I never had any direct run-ins with the Christian Knights, but there long were rumors they were still holding "cross lightings" deep in the woods and preparing for a violent race war. The group was active when I graduated from Davidson College in 1995. That year, they torched a hundred-year-old South Carolina black church, Macedonia Baptist. The Southern Poverty Law Center sued the Christian Knights on the church's behalf and secured a $37.8 million verdict, which was reduced to a still eye-popping $21.5 million. It was the case that turned Alabama attorney Morris Dees into a civil rights icon and effectively put that branch of the Klan out of business.

The white Evangelical Christians with whom I attended church will likely be offended by this chapter, because I know and they know that they would have helped me defend my family if the Klan ever made good on some of the threats the Klan sent me while I was a columnist for the (Myrtle Beach) *Sun News*. Plenty of white people throughout American history have been compelled by their Christianity to fight for racial equality. A fair number were willing to die for the cause, and did. Still, the name of that group—the *Christian* Knights of the Ku Klux Klan—speaks volumes about the disturbing, long-term relationship between American Christianity and racism. The white Evangelical Christian alliance with Trump is just the latest iteration of that truth.

FOR MOST OF MY FORTY-SEVEN YEARS OF LIFE, I've been in the presence of white Evangelical Christians who profess loyalty to Jesus and allegiance to the Confederate flag. I attended a mostly white Evangelical church for nearly two decades. I had convinced myself the white pastor was trying to move himself, and his parishioners, beyond racism and that I, his black brother in Christ, was obligated to help. He had rapped with a black teenager, invited black men into his pulpit, and thundered that white people needed to check their racist pasts. I needed to support him, to be a bridge to others like him. I didn't waver from that position even when my concerns about the church's forever all-white leadership were waved away with a "We'll hire a black pastor only if God tells us to. We don't make decisions based on race."

My faith remained until the pastor reduced me to just another race-baiter. After I explained why I thought he had unwisely scuttled a race relations group I was leading—the conversations had gotten difficult and uncomfortable, a necessary step before a deeper bond could take hold, something I made him aware of at the outset— he quickly put me in my place.

"I'm about Jesus, Issac," he told me. "You're just about race."

It didn't matter that I had dedicated myself to being in his church—and was raising my kids there and spent years defending him and his white congregants against charges of racism. At the end, when I refused to let things be, he came to see me as just another black man complaining and obsessing about race and unfairly burdening hardworking, God-fearing, Christian white people doing their best to reconcile with uppity black people not grateful for the kindness white Christians had extended us.

In that church, my wife and I had presented a dilemma to many of our white counterparts. In their minds, *real* black people were always relying upon white people. Tracy and I were married with kids and had "respectable" jobs and a long list of impressive academic credentials. Our subjects and verbs were almost always in agreement. Tracy and I didn't seem black, they told us. Our presence didn't cause them to reconsider their stereotypical views of black people. Instead, they put my wife and me into an ill-defined category and held fast to what they had long believed about black people.

Through it all, I stayed in that church, for nearly two decades. The good far outweighed the bad, I kept telling myself, trying to make peace with my decision. It was never easy.

The church's youth pastors, a married couple, invited Tracy and me to dinner. We had gone to dinner before.

They had visited our house; we had visited theirs. Our children had played with each other as we talked about the joys and frustrations of parenting and the craziness of the world and cracked jokes about nothing and everything. Sometimes we discussed race. They told me about an overbearing neighbor who would ask to borrow their car and not refill the tank or offer as much as a thank-you. That neighbor would ask to borrow money but never repay, would expect them to babysit her kids with no reciprocation. Because of white guilt or a misapplication of the "love thy neighbor" biblical command, they felt saying no to that neighbor would have been wrong, maybe even meant they were racist.

"How would you handle it if she was white?" I asked.

"I would tell her no more," the wife told me.

"Then why aren't you telling *her* no?"

So they did, their neighbor essentially responding with an "Okay, no biggie."

It was one of the typical ways I saw white Evangelical Christians in the South struggle with race, jumping from one extreme to the other, depending on the day or most recent sermon. Some days, they prostrated themselves before black people for the sin of racism and slavery. That often led to a short-term urgency to resolve racial differences that would produce interracial dinners and cookouts. White church members, including those youth pastors, hosted spa days for black single mothers and led school supply drives for poor black children. Some visited prisons. Others attended race relations workshops I facilitated. Those events would lead to a flood of tears and more Thank You Jesuses.

There would be pronouncements about how God had made such things—black people and white people eating fried fish and drinking sweet tea together—possible in a way that would not have been without divine intervention. I doubt neither the sincerity of their tears nor their motives. Their efforts for racial harmony also included events that were neither public nor publicized. During early morning, weekday hour-long prayer sessions, a handful of white church members genuinely prayed for Obama. In a region in which many white Evangelical Christians scanned the Bible to find verses to explain why assassinating Obama would be God-ordained, that's no small thing.

On many other days, though, I watched them demand that black people prostrate themselves for the sin of not having risen above racism; that black people respect the Southern white Evangelical Christian love of the Confederacy; that black people become color-blind; and that black people rethink why we vote for Democrats who supposedly spit on the Bible with an embrace of gay marriage and a supposed penchant for killing babies in the womb. Black Southerners, particularly Christians, are more like conservatives than liberals on such issues. But most can't bring themselves to vote for the Republican Party. Racism is a political deal breaker for them, which it isn't for white Evangelical Christians.

Their spasmodic thinking on race is also why years after that unexpected dinner invitation, the husband asked if I supported Herman Cain during the 2012 Republican primary. Cain was a black conservative radio talk show host and an opponent of President Obama. He was of the pull-yourself-up-by-the-bootstraps school. I believe there is no such thing as a self-made man. He was among the most unserious of unserious men long before allegations of past sexual misconduct surfaced and ended his campaign. No one who had ever read a word I had written could have reasonably concluded that I would have supported a man like Cain. And yet, that white youth pastor, whom I spent all that intimate time with, expressed profound disappointment that I wouldn't. Why? Because he didn't realize he was reducing me to just my skin color. He thought he could use his support of Cain to rebuff any accusations that his complaints about Obama had anything to do with race. He wanted my approval. I refused to provide it.

They aren't racist. They don't believe themselves superior or want harm to be inflicted upon black people, or any people. If I was in need and they could help, they would come running, no matter how angry they'd get or offended they'd feel after reading these words challenging their core beliefs. They are walking racial contradictions, haphazard, imperfect advocates for racial equality at their best, unwitting supporters of racism and open bigotry at their worst. It means they are like many white American Christians who came before them and explains why white Christians, en masse, have never prioritized uprooting white supremacy.

They didn't prioritize racial equality during the founding of the United States. They didn't in the lead-up to the Civil War. They didn't when the Confederacy spawned the Klan or when white mob violence reversed hard-won gains briefly secured during Reconstruction. White churches, particularly in the South, were big advocates of Jim Crow laws and customs even as black churches were being burned and black Christians hanged from trees. The drug war that tore through black families and communities didn't convince white Evangelical Christians to finally take a firm stand against racism. They did not show the compassion for black drug addicts they now want for the white ones in their own communities and congregations.

To confront white Evangelical Christians with this well-documented history is to be tarred a race-baiter. It's a smear, just another way to elicit white guilt. I know this because that's the typical reaction I've gotten even when there was nothing confrontational about my confronting. The connection between Christianity and racism is often taken as a personal indictment among people who can (rightly) say their faith has repeatedly compelled some among them to treat black people well but (wrongly) say that means nothing they do can be considered as advancing white supremacy.

The presence of the Christian Knights of the Ku Klux Klan and other overt white supremacist groups prevents many white Christians from committing to a true self-examination. Because they are not like the Klan, they reject charges of racism out of hand. The Klan's presence has convinced them that they are the real victims of racial slights. It's one of the reasons they embraced Trump. He spoke to their frustrations. His overt bigotry led them to believe that obviously bigoted and racist acts and words are neither bigoted nor racist. They aren't like the Klan; they aren't as crude as Trump. And he's just a God-sent tool protecting them from unfair accusations of racism.

When Trump called most Mexican immigrants rapists and drug dealers, many of the white Evangelical Christians I know decided to do the same. They began ignoring Jesus's admonition to treat the foreigner with kindness and compassion. In the Trump era, white Evangelical Christians now oppose the presence of refugees more than any other group. When Trump called African countries and Haiti "shitholes," many of the white Evangelical Christians I know began calling them shitholes, too. They felt freed from societal restraints that have never restrained Trump. Four years earlier, the youth pastor who unexpectedly invited me to dinner had hoped Herman Cain would serve that purpose. Trump did not lead white Evangelical Christians to this place. They were waiting to follow anyone who would take the first step.

But years before Trump came down that golden escalator, that youth pastor invited me and Tracy to that unexpected dinner. It began like our other dinners, with small talk and the saying of grace before we tore into the bread and biscuits. Then it got a little awkward.

"Some people are talking, and they are uncomfortable with you teaching the children," the pastor said. "We have to ask you to stop teaching in Kids' Church."

I was being banned from teaching Bible stories to elementary-age kids, as well as from rocking babies in the nursery to let their mamas and daddies listen in peace to the pastor delivering his sermon. I wasn't a pedophile. It was my views about race and sexuality that made me a threat to the sensibilities of little white Christian children with whom I never had discussed those subjects. A couple of Sundays a month, I would lead them in songs like "The Battle of Jericho." *"Joshua fought the battle of Jericho, Jericho, Jericho. Joshua fought the battle of Jericho, and the walls came tumbling down,"* we'd sing and laugh and dance before I had them settle into small plastic chairs to snack on dry Cheerios and grapes and listen to preselected Bible lessons.

I had already cut back my activity in the church after the pastor said I was just about race. I had stopped leading race relations discussions or examining the church's leadership structure. I quietly swallowed the indignity of being banished from teaching kids, and dutifully parked myself back in the congregation during the next Sunday morning worship services.

I stayed because of what I've come to see as black guilt. There's much discussion about white guilt, white people made to feel bad about the sins of their ancestors and obligated to make amends for things they did not do. Black guilt is something unique to black people in Trumpland. We—black Christians in the South in particular—feel obligated to alleviate the white guilt of our white Christian friends and neighbors, and to protect them from overly broad charges of racism from those who don't know them as well as we do. We see them in their full complexity, their full humanity. We know they aren't the walking stereotypes some believe they are. On many social issues, there is less divide between us and them than between us and black and white liberals in the North. It's not odd for some of our family members, or theirs, to live in brick homes on big lots, and some in trailer parks down the road. I grew up wearing oil-stained T-shirts to the IGA grocery store to get a fried pork chop sandwich lunch during breaks from rebuilding car engines or picking tobacco or tarring roofs, just as they did. They loved NASCAR. My stepfather was a stock car driver. We gathered around the TV every Friday night, like our white Evangelical counterparts, to watch *The Dukes of Hazzard*, which starred a Confederate-flag-draped orange car named *General Lee*.

Those common experiences blinded us to larger realities, or at least had a way of softening us to day-to-day racial tensions. Though we worked in the same fields, they had more land, passed down from generations and supported by national and local policies that helped grow the white middle class while stunting the black middle class. Their schools weren't as great as many in the North, but they made sure we remained relegated to the poorest, most segregated ones. We worked side by side in the same factories, but they made sure they got the best jobs and the biggest salaries. In the white Evangelical church where I had my children dedicated, they maintained most of the control. They decided when the racial discussions had gone "too far." They decided which visiting black preacher was acceptable enough to give a sermon. They decided what racial harmony meant, and it was often about appearances, interracial lunches and dinners, and hugs and prayer groups, not the gritty, grimy work of ensuring racial equality. They determined who was civil, mostly prioritizing their own comfort above all else.

That's why it grates on me like little else to hear white liberals and moderates wax poetic about why people like me need to commit to listening to white Evangelical Christians, as though the real problem is that white Evangelical Christians have been silenced for far too long, and that's why they turned to a bigot like Trump. Those white liberals and moderates haven't been in the trenches as I've been in the trenches. And yet, they've felt confident enough, from afar, to tell me why white Evangelical Christians turned to Trump, and why people like me need to accept it in good faith.

I'll tell you why they turned to Trump: because Christianity as practiced in America has never been incompatible with white supremacy. Pretending that they turned to him because of a supposed "economic angst," which black people in Trumpland suffer from far more than white people here, or because they feel their religious rights are under attack—even as they feel comfortable with the racial inequities in their midst from which they daily benefit—helps no one. That's why it grates on me like little else to hear white liberals and moderates commit to honoring the voices of white people in Trumpland while telling black people to just shut up and take it.

One of the unacknowledged truths of diversity is that living among those unlike you won't automatically lead to enlightened views. Diversity is not enough. White people are expert at compartmentalizing when it comes to race. It's why they can love and respect individual black people while despising or misunderstanding black people in general. It's why the "I have a black friend" defense is nonsensical. My white brothers and sisters in Christ chose Trump and his bigotry over us—not because they had to, but because they wanted to. All those years spent earnestly engaging them on their own terms in their own homes in their own church did not dissuade them from making that choice.

The Sensible Paranoia
of Black People in Trumpland

HE TAPPED ME ON THE ARM as I was jotting down contact information for people standing in the parking lot of Conway Medical Center near Myrtle Beach, South Carolina, on a late Friday afternoon, doing my due diligence as a journalist who may want to speak with them again.

"Excuse me, sir," he said while holding the hand of a young boy who was about as tall as my inquisitor's thigh. "I don't mean to be disrespectful or nothing like that. But before you ask for my information, I need to know something. Do you really give a fuck about this? Do you really give a fuck about us?"

On the third floor in a bed in the critical care unit of that hospital lay his twenty-five-year-old brother, a man named Christopher Bennett. He was brain-dead. All that day, doctors had been urging family members to take him off life support. All that day, family members refused. They did not trust the doctors. They did not trust the gaggle of police officers who had gathered in that hospital the night before when Bennett was rushed into the emergency room from the J. Reuben Long Detention Center. They did not trust anything they were being told by anyone. Another family member had been found dead in a cell in the same jail months earlier. Officials say it was from natural causes; the family isn't so sure.

How had Bennett, a healthy twenty-five-year-old at eight that Thursday night before, ended up brain-dead just a couple of hours later? Police officers in several cars from multiple agencies, including the area's drug enforcement unit, pulled him over for allegedly veering left of the center line in his Dodge Charger and took him to the jail. Why had Bennett's family gotten a panicked call from an inmate who said he saw guards pull Bennett's all-but-lifeless body from his cell by his feet? Didn't someone claim Bennett had banged his head against the cell wall for a half hour? Or was it that no one had known he had been unresponsive in his cell for that long?

Why did Bennett have a black eye and a missing tooth? Why was his spleen damaged? Why had a doctor they couldn't name called his grandmother to say Bennett had been beaten? Didn't someone say something about an injury to his spine, too? A family member took a peek below a towel wrapped around Bennett's neck and upper body and spotted scratches and bruises. Who or what caused those? Why were they told not to take photos of the then-brain-dead Bennett (though they did anyway)?

Those questions were shooting rapid fire through the brains of family members and friends waiting impatiently in the ICU waiting room and in the hospital's parking lot. Such questions by black people are common here in Trumpland. In this place, you never know when race or racism is at play, and the default is to be suspicious, particularly when white cops and white doctors are telling you not to be. It isn't because we are paranoid; it's because we've seen too much, because our parents and grandparents suffered too much, often in silence. And we know, better than our supposed white liberal allies in the North and elsewhere, that it's logical to assume the worst first, even if we sometimes end up being wrong. We went from literal shackles and horsewhips on the back to a century of lynching and white mobs violently overturning black progress. You don't forget the image of black bodies being burned alive in the town square or dangling from trees as white people gathered around to cheer, even if it was your grandma or aunt, not you, who had firsthand knowledge of such evils.

We came home from World War II after helping save the world from Hitler to Jim Crow laws and customs and being targeted by white mobs afraid we'd demand the equality and respect we experienced overseas. We had the Tuskegee experiment inflicted upon us. We were experimented on in prisons. We were stolen from Southern streets—by the hundreds of thousands—brought up on charges for things like spitting on the sidewalk, and essentially sold by the American criminal *justice* system to large corporations where we were worked literally to death.

We've had white people enjoy our music in our juke joints only to have Klan-hooded white people shoot up the place and torture us for the sin of having a good time in ways they didn't like. We were criminalized for the sin of becoming addicted to heroin and crack cocaine. We largely missed the initial opioid crisis because doctors wouldn't prescribe us those pills: they thought we were drug dealers, or that our dark skin made us less susceptible to pain. We've watched a black man be shot by a white cop five times in the back as that black man ran away—then watched as a jury refused to find the cop guilty even after seeing clear video of the entire scene unfolding.

Listen. Where we live, white people used chains—yes, long, thick metal chains—to mark the spot where they would allow us to swim in the Atlantic, the very ocean where they dragged us from Africa in one of history's most horrific journeys. That's why when we ask questions that sound like conspiracy theories, maybe it's best to listen and try to understand rather than ridicule. That's why when we wonder if what a white colleague said or a white pastor preached or a white cop demanded has something to do with our race, we are being neither hypersensitive nor unreasonable, just prudent.

We've had white friends and colleagues tell us to shut up when we've faced discrimination in ways large and small because they simply couldn't believe it could be true. We know our jails and prisons—and our special-ed classrooms—are filled with people who look like us. We know the truth of what famed Republican political strategist Lee Atwater said, that though openly calling us *nigger* fell out of style in the South beginning sometime in the 1960s, they just found other ways to do it anyway. Because we know all of this, it's not paranoid to suspect that we are being lied to by the police after yet another one of us is found dead in a jail cell. Unless, of course, you believe we are the only group on the planet that doesn't learn from our experiences.

"Do you really give a fuck about us?" the young man asked as respectfully and calmly as a man can ask such a question.

We were standing in a county in which Donald Trump received nearly 70 percent of the vote, where the drug enforcement unit not too long before had lied about why they had shot a small-time drug dealer, paralyzing him for life, and nobody cared.

"Do you really give a fuck about us?"

Those words stuck with me as I drove home after having watched Bennett's mother, who had just been released from jail after being charged in a domestic dispute, crying uncontrollably on a bench near the hospital's entrance. The image of a mama felled by overwhelming pain cut deeper as the words of his fiancée—the mother of four of his children, including a one-month-old—cut deeper still.

"My kids' father is never coming home," Scarlet Russell told me.

Instead of a wedding, she would attend his funeral a few days later.

By that Friday afternoon, after checking with a few of my law enforcement and medical sources, I had gotten a sense of what the official story about Bennett's death would be. An initial investigation would determine there had been no foul play. Officials who had seen video from inside the vehicle that transported Bennett would say he looked fine during the ride and check-in at the jail.

Bennett would die late that Saturday morning. That night, a white constable in a neighboring county was on a ride-along with police who stopped a black man because that black man had also allegedly crossed the center line on the road. Police said they smelled marijuana. The man refused to get out of the car, then quickly backed up, hitting a police cruiser. The constable shot the man eight times, claiming he had almost gotten run over—which is not what video of the incident showed.

By Tuesday, results from a preliminary autopsy on Bennett's body would determine there were no signs of trauma. My sources wouldn't go into details then, though they told me what they expected the toxicology results to say once they were released, that his death was drug-related. Maybe, in an effort to avoid detection, he consumed an enormous amount of drugs when he was stopped. He had had run-ins with the police before, including for drugs.

Maybe he overdosed in his cell and hit his head on something hard as he fell to the floor. He was brain-dead because by the time his unresponsive body was found and CPR was initiated, oxygen had been cut off from his brain for too long. An autopsy report would later suggest something similar. That's why police officers were adamant about one thing, that Bennett had not been beaten, even though several members of his family and close friends suspected he had been.

"First it was an 'extremely serious head injury,'" Dinedra Smith said. "Now it's 'no signs of trauma.' How? What sense does that make?"

It was Smith who called me early that Friday morning.

"Do you know anyone around here willing to write about police beating a young man and now he's on life support?" she asked. "It's my brother-in-law."

Smith has reason to be skeptical of official police accounts. Her brother, Jamar Huggins, is serving a fifteen-year-sentence in a Columbia, South Carolina, prison for a home invasion in which he was most likely not involved. It did not matter that Smith and other family members spent years hosting vigils and peaceful protests and launching petitions and online campaigns and scraping together thousands of dollars to pay for lawyers to try to get Huggins out. It did not matter if truth was on their side because when it comes to young black men and the criminal justice system, nothing matters—except that they should be presumed guilty.

Smith knew that though the police report in the Bennett case described a chance meeting, a routine traffic stop between Bennett and the drug enforcement unit, that wasn't the whole story. The DEU had been trailing Bennett for days, if not weeks. According to his grandmother, the unit was trying to recruit Bennett to serve as a confidential informant. When he kept refusing, they kept following him and his friends and brothers. Hours before Bennett was stopped that final time, cops paraded in front of their house, passing by in their cars and circling back multiple times. Bennett's brothers and friends say they never report such harassment, or times they've been roughed up, because it would be a waste of energy. Who would believe them? Some of them have convictions. They live in what police have deemed a "known drug area." They are the *thugs*. Constitutional protections aren't for people like *them*.

President Trump told police officers to not be too nice to young men like them. Trump's supporters here, including white Evangelical Christians, either cheered him on or said that they wish he "wouldn't say things like that" while still defending him from charges of racism. Then–Attorney General Jeff Sessions pulled back on Obama-era efforts to hold police accountable for wrongdoing and told prosecutors to reignite the war on drugs. Those young men, like the one who asked if I gave a fuck, know that's how they are viewed. They knew that, even as police officers, jail officials, and coroners tried to convince them to believe the official account of why a young man they loved died. They also knew that SLED, the law enforcement agency responsible for investigating such deaths, has had a spotty track record when it comes to holding law enforcement officials to account.

They knew about the story of a black man, Johnny Jermaine Rush, on the other side of the state line who was walking home from work late one night. He was harassed and beaten by a police officer who had stopped him for jaywalking—and that beating reached the public's attention only because an anonymous whistleblower released video of the arrest to a newspaper. (The officer avoided jail time by benefiting from a restorative justice program most black men who commit violent crimes have not been allowed to use. He received twelve months of probation and community service, and his record could be expunged.) They knew about Freddie Gray and how people around the country were more upset with the resulting protests than with reports of a special police unit in Baltimore robbing residents and planting drugs and shooting and framing them with "drop" guns.

They knew that as they made funeral arrangements, prosecutors in Louisiana were announcing there would be no charges in the shooting death of Alton Sterling. They knew of the intense protests going on in Sacramento in the aftermath of yet another black man shot to death by police, that one occurring in his grandma's backyard. They know if you wear dark skin, you are more likely to be depicted by media outlets in the most unflattering ways, even as young white men who shoot up schools and plant bombs are treated as full, complex human beings.

Conservatives would tell them to buck up and stop complaining because, statistically speaking, young black men, unarmed or not, are rarely killed by police. Such incidents total in the hundreds every year. Besides, they are more likely to be killed by other young black men. It's akin to telling black people that there was no reason to oppose lynchings in the twentieth-century United States. Such events numbered in the low thousands over the course of a century, making them, statistically speaking, even rarer than police shootings in the twenty-first century. Never mind that the killings themselves are awful, or that the specter of millions of white Americans either cheering the killers or looking the other way rubs salt in those still all-too-fresh racial wounds. It's even worse when that uncritical support of law enforcement ensures that cops who do dastardly things on the job are rarely charged or convicted.

Then there's the seminal study from Harvard University of twenty million children documenting how even black men from rich families are arrested at rates greater than white boys from poor families, undercutting the theory growing more popular in liberal circles that it's all about income, not race.

Those young black men are frequently told their concerns are overblown, that cops need to be praised, not scrutinized, that families like theirs are solely to blame for the chaos with which they daily have to contend. Why should they believe police officers and others who claim their brother, their friend, effectively caused his own death, even if those officials are telling the truth? Didn't they say the same about Trayvon Martin, and suggest that

Freddie Gray somehow broke his own neck, that Eric Garner died not because of an illegal chokehold, but because he was too fat?

"Do you really give a fuck about us?"

In Trumpland, I'm not convinced we do.

Black Voters and White Voters

IMAGINE LOUIS FARRAKHAN RAN FOR PRESIDENT. Imagine he received a record level of black support in the general election after having garnered strong support from them during the primaries. Imagine that black people were the main reason Farrakhan had become president of the United States. Now imagine how the (mostly white) mainstream would have explained such a result.

They would not have made excuses for black voters. They would not have said it was reasonable for black voters to have put an anti-Semite in charge of laws that would affect Jewish Americans because of the "economic angst" black people have felt forever in this country. They would not have told Jews to empathize more with the black voters who elevated open, brazen anti-Semitism into the most powerful office in the world. They would not have launched a thousand stories from black barbershops and beauty salons assuring Jewish people that black people really weren't anti-Semitic even though they widely supported an anti-Semite the way they launched a thousand stories from out-of-the-way diners to humanize white Trump supporters.

I cannot imagine voting for a man like Farrakhan, then demanding that my Jewish friends and neighbors understand my choice. I'd be embarrassed. I'd feel like a fraud, as though I had betrayed them because I was scared or just didn't care as much about them as I had long let on. I say this as a man who understands the gut affinity of a man like Donald Trump to white people and Farrakhan to black people. Farrakhan was pro-black when it wasn't popular. Farrakhan, as much as he is rightly despised for his anti-Semitism, homophobia, and misogyny, has a track record of black uplift in some Northeastern cities. And as much as I don't like to admit it, he was partly responsible for one of the most important days of my early life, the 1995 Million Man March. I needed that event like I needed oxygen.

I was desperate for a reason to believe in the beauty of black people again. I had recently graduated from a prestigious, nearly all-white private Southern liberal arts college—one I chose in large part because I was unsure about black excellence and thought competing against top-level white students would erase that doubt. I would either prove black students like me were good enough, or that we weren't. I proved we were, but I left Davidson College with a significant number of psychic scars. That came on the heels of my being too ashamed to mention during my time as a Davidson student that my hero big brother was languishing in a South Carolina prison serving a life sentence for first-degree murder. I was ashamed of having grown up in a home in which my father beat my mother. I wanted none of my white Davidson classmates, or even the black, Latino, Native American, or Asian ones, to know that my youngest brothers had begun getting into serious trouble as well.

All of that made me feel as though black wasn't beautiful. In stepped Farrakhan trying to coax a million black men to the nation's capital, not to ask white people for anything, but to be better men, more responsible fathers, husbands worthy of the love and respect of their wives. We were to atone for our sins, for not keeping our communities strong. That message resonated with me and many other black people in South Carolina, who chartered buses to DC for the march the way so many had when Dr. Martin Luther King Jr. held the March on Washington for Jobs and Freedom on that same ground thirty-two years earlier.

I wish someone other than Farrakhan had made the call. Though his anti-Semitism is better known today, he has always been a controversial figure. I did not learn much about Farrakhan when I was a student at Davidson. I only knew of him through sound bites and rumors from black classmates and friends from St. Stephen, South Carolina. But there was no secret about who he was even then for those willing to look. Three years before the Million Man March, when I was a sophomore at Davidson, the renowned Harvard University professor Henry Louis

Gates Jr. penned a piece in the *New York Times* titled "Black Demagogues and Pseudo-Scholars." He argued that there was an urgency for black people to speak forthrightly against the anti-Semitism within their ranks and cited Farrakhan's Nation of Islam as one of the most prominent sources of such anti-Semitism. In 1991, Farrakhan wrote a two-volume book called *The Secret Relationship Between Blacks and Jews*, in which he asserted that Jews were major players in the Atlantic slave trade. The American Historical Association quickly pointed out why that was an anti-Semitic lie based on egregiously flawed scholarship. I was graduating from high school that year and heard nothing about the controversy at the time.

Gates knew, which is why he wrote this for the *New York Times*:

> But why target the Jews? Using the same historical methodology, after all, the researchers of the book could have produced a damning treatise on the involvement of left-handers in the "black holocaust." The answer requires us to go beyond the usual shibboleths about bigotry and view the matter, from the demagogues' perspective, strategically: as the bid of one black elite to supplant another.
>
> It requires us, in short, to see anti-Semitism as a weapon in the raging battle of who will speak for black America—those who have sought common cause with others or those who preach a barricaded withdrawal into racial authenticity.
>
> The strategy of these apostles of hate, I believe, is best understood as ethnic isolationism—they know that the

more isolated black America becomes, the greater their power. And what's the most efficient way to begin to sever black America from its allies? Bash the Jews, these demagogues apparently calculate, and you're halfway there.

It's an uncomfortable truth that that was the man who brought Black America together in such large numbers. In the black community, he has always been something of an enigma. He's despised in some quarters for his suspected role in the murder of Malcolm X, and in others for his bombastic speeches and tendency to speak poorly of black Christians and others not in favor of his plan for racial separation. Many white supremacists respect Farrakhan because his rhetoric about black people, and the solution to the race problem, frequently echoes theirs. When white supremacists approve of what someone is preaching, it should give us pause. That's why the Million Man March, a call to strengthen the black community, was not universally praised by black people. While a young Barack Obama attended, Representative John Lewis, an icon of the civil rights era, declined to participate because Farrakhan "preached racial, religious and sexual divisiveness," the *Atlanta Journal-Constitution* wrote.

I felt I had no choice but to go despite my distaste and disdain for Farrakhan. Once there, one scene stood out among everything else. There was a woman, a black woman. She was lying on her back on a blanket in the grass. Her eyes were closed. Her legs were bent and crossed at the knees. Her skin glistened in the sunlight. She may have been a decade older than I was. I can't remember if her arms were resting underneath her head like a pillow, but I believe they were. Maybe she was dreaming. Or maybe she was just deeply inhaling the music and the moment. Whatever she was doing, it was obvious she felt safe in a sea of strange black men. I don't know if she had come alone, but it didn't matter. Every black man near her was unofficially standing guard. Had anyone dared try to disturb her, to take advantage of her, to disrespect her, they would have had to navigate a phalanx of black men determined to answer Farrakhan's call to be better men. No one was going to hurt that beautiful black woman with those men around.

I had never seen anything like it. I had never been more proud, or moved. Though I knew that was not the way black men always treated black women, it lifted my spirits. It convinced me that black could be—and was—beautiful. Since then, anytime thoughts of black people being ugly or unkind or violent invade my mind, I've been able to tap back into that scene to flush those dark thoughts out. I didn't stay the entire day. My brother Willie and I left as soon as Farrakhan climbed the stage and began to speak several hours into the event. I didn't go to see Farrakhan. I didn't want to hear anything he had to say. I went to see that black woman lying there in peace surrounded by black men ready to care for her. I went to see black men bump into each other and accidentally scruff up each other's brand-new sneakers and say "my bad" and "no problem" instead of allowing such slights to devolve into angry confrontations. I went because I needed an image to counter that of me and my friends running from a black fraternity party in Charlotte because someone pulled out a gun.

I wish that one of the most important days of my life wasn't linked to Farrakhan. It is. I wish I could say he played no role in restoring my faith in black people. He did. I want to tell you that I'm not conflicted about that truth. I am.

I DON'T NEED TO BE LECTURED about the need to understand white Trump voters, because I already understand. I get that life often presents dilemmas, particularly when it comes to race. Just as I was conflicted about an event pulled together by a man like Farrakhan, I understand why some Trump voters are conflicted about him. And black people are not perfect vessels.

Too many of us cheered when O. J. Simpson beat double-murder charges, not caring that meant dancing on the graves of two young white people who were violently taken from this earth. That the celebration was purportedly about a black man finally besting a criminal justice system that has for too long victimized us and was not necessarily about a black man getting away with murder is no excuse. It was wrong. It was unseemly, shortsighted—cruel. We could have used Simpson's acquittal to highlight all the ways the system can, and has, gotten it wrong, often to the detriment of black families and communities. We didn't, letting a critical opportunity to build alliances that could have led to real change slip through our fingers. O.J., a man who spent much of his adult life insisting he wanted nothing to do with blackness, his or anyone else's, became a de facto hero to Black America in a way he never had with his Hertz commercials. We don't need heroes like him but sometimes foolishly embrace them anyway.

Al Sharpton was an unofficial civil rights adviser to the White House during the Obama era despite his controversial track record on race, which included his role in perpetrating a hoax by a young black girl against six white men she falsely accused of an assault. (Full disclosure: I once made an appearance on his MSNBC politics show.) He played a prominent role in the 1991 Crown Heights riots. He led protesters through the streets who were shouting anti-Semitic epithets during a period in which a rabbinical student was stabbed by a group of young black men after a Hasidic driver killed a seven-year-old black boy. Sharpton has come a long way since his worst days. He is more likely to preach racial unity and understanding than repeat his worst mistakes. For that he should be credited. If I believe in redemption even for white people who have hurt black people—and I do—I can't argue against Sharpton's. But the black community's complicated relationship with someone like Sharpton should not be sidestepped just because it's inconvenient.

Black activists, students, and protesters, along with white liberal allies, hit another low when they rushed to condemn white Duke University lacrosse players accused of raping a black stripper. In that case, a white prosecutor in Durham, North Carolina, hoping to get reelected, was using righteous black anger to inflict a profound injustice upon privileged young white men. What happened there should not be excused just because those young white men had powerful parents and lawyers in their corner. They were able to avoid the prison sentences suffered by the young black and Latino boys of "the Central Park Five" infamy. They, too, were falsely accused of a brutal gang rape, in Central Park. In response, Donald Trump took out expensive newspaper ads to call for the reimposition of the death penalty in New York. Even after those young men were fully exonerated when the real rapist came forward and his confession was confirmed by DNA evidence, Trump continued condemning the young men. Many New York police officers and former prosecutors still call them rapists. Those black and Latino young men had it much worse than the falsely accused white Duke lacrosse players. Nonetheless, what happened at Duke was disturbing, and not enough people apologized or tried to make amends for their role in that chaos.

Despite a deep dive by the Justice Department under Obama that determined there was little evidence that Michael Brown had his arms raised when he was killed by officer Darren Wilson, the "hands up, don't shoot" chant remains a staple at some protests. It wasn't enough that DOJ had found massive, widespread civil rights abuses and violations perpetrated by the Ferguson police department against black residents—kindling the spark that was Brown's death, which led to several days of sometimes violent unrest. Sometimes black people are among those quickest to rush to judgment about ill-defined incidents, only parts of which are revealed in video snippets on social media. Many innocent people have had their lives and reputations ruined that way, often without apology even after the truth is revealed. That's no small thing. And some of us aren't as forthright today when we talk about the danger of men like Farrakhan as we need to be, which is why a prominent black woman organizer of the Women's March in 2017 had to step down. She just couldn't renounce Farrakhan.

I get it. We all have racially problematic skeletons in our closet. On that count, Trump supporters are not unique. None of us is above reproach on an issue so emotional, complex, vexing, and ever-evolving as race in the United States of America. But Trump's presence in office underscores why it is unwise to pretend all racially problematic decisions are equally harmful or derive from the same place, because they aren't. The imbalance in power is real. That imbalance means some racial mistakes and missteps will cause greater harm than others. Though white Trump supporters and apologists use the examples I listed above as a way to absolve themselves of guilt or to downplay what the presence of a man like Trump in the White House really means in a diversifying nation, the rest of us shouldn't.

I went to the Million Man March, not to hate white people, but to learn to love black people. I would not have excused—and still won't excuse—any ugly, anti-Semitic, or homophobic thing Farrakhan has ever said, or ever will. A man like him would never receive my vote, not even for dogcatcher, let alone the presidency. It's not a close call. On that score, there is no confliction. That would be true even if my choices boiled down to Farrakhan versus someone like Mike Huckabee or Sarah Palin. I know that's true of the overwhelming majority of black voters. Because in 2004, we ran a kind of experiment.

Farrakhan wasn't on the ballot trying to secure the Democratic presidential nomination; Sharpton was. It was a year in which the nomination was up for grabs. There was no Democratic incumbent. The Democratic base despised President George W. Bush and was looking for a different kind of candidate to challenge him. Sharpton thought maybe he could do what Jesse Jackson had done in the 1980s and, if not able to win, at least be competitive and win a few contests. He did poorly in the three early states—overwhelmingly white Iowa and New Hampshire and more diverse Nevada—barely registering in the vote totals. Then came South Carolina, where black people were expected to cast 50 to 60 percent of the vote in the Democratic primary.

Sharpton decided it would be in that state he would plant his flag, given the large black vote. He talked about doing well enough there to secure enough delegates to have a say on the floor during the Democratic National

Convention. Instead, he came in a distant third place behind two white men, well behind John Kerry, the eventual nominee, and John Edwards, a native South Carolinian. Few national political analysts took note of that outcome. They weren't surprised Sharpton failed to gain political traction. His candidacy was a long shot from the outset, a kind of protest campaign. But those political analysts overlooked the significance of that message and have yet to reexamine the outcome even in the wake of a Trump presidency. If what those analysts were saying about why poor and middle-class white people chose Trump— economic angst, feeling silenced and overlooked, anger, feeling put upon by those who don't understand and ridicule them—was true, why didn't that translate into a better showing for Sharpton among black voters in 2004? I say it's because black people are comfortable choosing white candidates over black ones, and because black people would not elevate a man they knew white people viewed as a racial demagogue into the White House.

That's true even though Sharpton had spent years speaking up for downtrodden black people before he ran for the presidency. Sharpton preached in black churches since he was a young boy, about black uplift, about black power, about black excellence. He participated in and sometimes led vital civil rights and antidiscrimination protests. He founded the National Action Network to nationalize those efforts, an organization that routinely hosts top Democratic presidential candidates today. I was there when he showed up at a Cracker Barrel restaurant in little-known Murrells Inlet, South Carolina, to support our mutual friend, Rose Rock, mother of famed comedian Chris Rock. She felt discriminated against while being served in the restaurant. Sharpton flew in from New York to lend his voice to her cause.

If what national political analysts said about why white people chose Trump made sense—even though Trump had never done for downtrodden white people what Sharpton had done for downtrodden black people—it would make even more sense for black voters to have chosen Sharpton. And yet, when Sharpton threw his hat in the ring, black people looked elsewhere. They were not going to ignore his problematic past and his ill-fitting qualifications for the office, or prioritize their personal pain. Besides, even if every black person decided to stand behind Sharpton, it likely still would not have been enough to make him the Democratic nominee, let alone the president. That's why black activists frequently say that black people can't be racist, because we don't have enough collective power, even if individual black people can do racist things. Had Farrakhan run, black voters would have ignored him, too, and more decisively.

But when a demagogue like Trump ran for the presidency after spending five years promoting a bigoted conspiracy theory about the nation's first black president, 58 percent of white voters jumped on board, just enough to put him over the top. That's not akin to making *The Apprentice* a top-rated show on NBC or ignoring his amorality to chuckle at his bluster about his supposed high intellect and riches. Neither is it like black rappers emulating his braggadocio style, valuing sizzle over substance. Those amount to little more than guilty pleasures that didn't hurt the already vulnerable.

To make a bigoted man president is to inflict his bigotry upon black and brown communities, no matter the reason you choose to support him. That's what Trump voters did, including a majority of middle-class and wealthy white Americans, not just the poor whites who have received so much attention. They did not care that they were inflicting Trump upon black and brown communities. They only cared about themselves and what they might get out of the deal.

Black people are imperfect, too. But there are some racial lines black voters wouldn't cross. The reason Democrats have not—and would not—elect a man like Trump, or a black demagogue like Farrakhan, is because black people wouldn't let them.

In 2016, Republicans proved they had no such racial constraints, because White America was comfortable crossing a racist line. That they stuck with Trump through his first term despite the ugly things Trump kept saying and doing says they still don't get it. I'm losing hope they ever will.

The Never-Ending Quest to Comfort
White People in Trumpland

THE BLACK-AND-WHITE IMAGE was of a crudely drawn, savage-looking, kinky-haired, emaciated black man dressed like Tarzan. He was sitting on a beach, apparently somewhere in Africa. It came with this caption: "Ever hear blacks refer to their 'rich African heritage?' Let's have a look…" The large bone through the man's large nose was labeled "African fashion," the straw hut behind him "African architecture," a shellfish impaled by a spear "African cuisine" and "African invention," respectively. A single finger-drawn line in the sand was "African literature."

"Can you name any African philosophers?" it asked.

It was one of the first pieces of reader hate mail I received after I began writing about race for the (Myrtle Beach) *Sun News*. It came in the form of a letter from a man calling himself John Macx, "Propaganda Deputy, Illinois KKK/Chicago Den." It was in response to columns in which I tried to empathize with white people. I revealed the irrational fear of black men I had been fighting for years in an effort to make them comfortable enough to admit theirs. I apologized to African slaves for once having been ashamed of them for reasons I still can't fully explain.

As a black lead columnist for a newspaper in Trumpland, I knew I had to pick my battles wisely. Focusing on the racists would leave me no time to think about anything else. I eventually threw away a large stack of hate mail that had been growing by the week. But I held onto the "African heritage" letter. It struck a nerve, not because there was any truth to it, but because growing up in the South, a part of me had been conditioned to believe there was.

IN JUNE 2019, I traveled to Ghana for the first time, the "Year of Return," which marked the four-hundredth anniversary of the first enslaved Africans shipped to what would become the United States. For most of my life, I wanted no connection to the dark continent. I had been convinced, by whom or what I don't precisely know, that the *American* in my African-American was better than the *African*. It didn't matter that I could trace my familial line directly to the race-based chattel slavery in the region of South Carolina where I was born and raised and still reside.

I can't tell you how I came to view Africa and my dark skin negatively. Maybe it grew from being taught from state-sanctioned history books in segregated schools that spoke of happy slaves, unsavory abolitionists, and heroic Confederate soldiers who were just trying to protect their homeland. Maybe it got rooted in when my oldest brother committed murder when I was a nine-year-old, linking in my mind *violent* and *black*. Maybe it was solidified by my sometimes-quiet acceptance of racial injustice and inequality inside newsrooms in an industry struggling with how best to reflect the nation's emerging diversity. I've had white colleagues in one breath say my writings about race were radical and irresponsible and in the next admit they had not bothered to study the racial history I was alluding to. No matter my nuance or depth of knowledge or their racial ignorance, they were "objective" and I wasn't.

The depth of the horror faced by generations of black people here is hard to fathom. It could come across as dystopic science fiction from a madman if you didn't know it was real. Who would think there was a time in Georgia a black woman named Mary Turner could have been lynched—burned alive, her fetus cut from her stomach and stomped on by her attackers—for the sin of wanting justice for her husband, who had also been lynched? Or that it would be done in public, with the full knowledge of local authorities and a gaggle of giddy white Christians? It's not just about my former white colleagues, white people in general, or the white mobs who arose every time black people made progress. It's about me, too, and my sometimes reluctance to speak racial truths I know will upset white people.

I understand why introducing white readers to facts they didn't want to be made aware of will discomfort them. That task is made more difficult when journalists are unwilling or unable to properly deal with racial tension within their orbits. Too many times, I didn't handle it properly. Too many times, I gave in and was weak when I needed to be steadfast.

I once wrote about a prominent white man in Myrtle Beach who lost a real estate case. He marched into my editor's office saying I was biased because the couple he lost to was black like me. Never mind that I had never met the couple and didn't know they were black. For all I knew, they were blue, which happened to be their last name. I wrote the story based on interviews with their white attorney and court documents. None of that mattered. My editors allowed him to write a long letter to the editor taking me to task—without naming a single factual error I had made—after they printed a lengthy "correction" to my article, which consisted of his side of the story, even though he had turned down my request for comment before the story was published. I stewed about the indignity but swallowed hard, as black people in Trumpland are taught to. I neither let on it bothered me nor spoke about it with my colleagues.

In another instance, as I was returning to my desk from lunch, my white publisher dressed me down in the newsroom for having written a column she didn't like.

A group of irate conservative, white readers had grown more boisterous and had been in her ear about me. They had been hounding her for weeks. They wanted me gone. It wasn't the first time a group of white readers wanted me disappeared from the newspaper, or at least neutered, and wouldn't be the last. But she was the first publisher I had who had decided to give in to the pressure. She called me and my editor to her office a couple of times to tell me to stop writing about race and politics the way I had been doing long before she was hired. The first meeting was a gentle demand; the second time she dropped the gentle. I left each one thinking I had to write the way I knew I should, that doing so could mean the end of my career at the *Sun News*, that doing anything else would be journalistically unethical. For the first time since I was a newbie journalist who believed my severe stutter would lead to my professional demise, I walked into the office every day thinking it might be my last and left every evening warning my wife that tomorrow might be the day.

Once again, I swallowed hard and did not let my colleagues in the newsroom know what was happening. I briefly let it slip during a conversation with a colleague in our DC bureau. He wanted to highlight it in a journalistic newsletter. I told him not to. He asked if he could do it anonymously. I still told him no. I still don't fully understand why. As journalists, we are to shine light in dark places, even if we happen to be in one of them. In that instance, I didn't. I failed. I think—*think*—a part of me wanted to protect her from charges of racism. She wasn't racist, isn't racist, but was giving in to readers trying to pressure a black man to either be less black or be out of a job. Some of those readers had begun sending me provocative, hateful email messages hoping I'd say something in response that could give my publisher cause to fire me. It should be noted that South Carolina is a so-called right to work state. Union membership is nearly nonexistent. Most of us don't work under contract. I didn't. There were no union protections to rely upon.

It's odd, I know. I was enduring her wrath but trying to protect her image. It's akin to what white journalists have been doing in the Trump era, protecting the image of those causing the most harm, perhaps out of a sense of guilt or obligation. Things went on that way seemingly forever, though probably only several months. As I was shielding my publisher from a public reckoning, I was publicly thanking the paper's mostly white readership for accepting me. Almost none of them had called me nigger, many supported me, and the "African heritage" hate mail letters were few and far between, I wrote. I also thanked the white editors who stood up for me during my toughest moments. I'd be greeted warmly at Republican political events by people with whom I strongly disagreed. They loved that I was outwardly loving toward the region and appreciative of the United States. They could use me to counter the white-hot, righteous black anger that was Reverend H. H. Singleton, the outspoken president of the local NAACP, with whom I sometimes clashed.

I was doing the dutiful thing many successful black Americans do, repeatedly paying public homage to the white people who had "given me an opportunity" and "allowed" me to use my skills. When white conservative readers created a loud chorus to punish me for being too black, I stoically, silently endured it. That was required of black people, I was taught while growing up in Trumpland. Though I had no say over what the ocean decided, I was to make no waves.

My publisher didn't stop until my reporting led to high-profile national writing awards, as well as a top journalistic prize from corporate executives, a real feat for a newspaper our size. Almost overnight, it was as though none of it had happened, she had backed off so suddenly and completely. She invited me to a Christmas party at her house. She told me to visit her in the new city where she eventually moved and said it would be great having me write for the newspaper she took over after leaving Myrtle Beach. (That didn't materialize. I took other writing and teaching jobs; they prioritized political coverage needs.)

There were many other slights I swallowed. After I began as the first black lead columnist for the only daily newspaper in Myrtle Beach, taking over for a beloved white columnist whose lighthearted take on politics had endeared him to many, I had to fight off attempts by my well-meaning white editors to "tone it down" a bit, the same editors who would later defend me against the publisher. They didn't want me to be seen as the "black columnist." They simply could not hear me when I repeatedly said there was nothing I could do about that. It was hard to get them to hear even when a few readers called in to say I was throwing a gang sign in the photo that accompanied my column, when all I had done was rest my chin between my thumb and index finger while staring into the camera. Other times, I had white colleagues—including those I frequently spoke in favor of during tense moments in the newsroom—tell me my opinions about race were suspect, and they said this in ways they would never use with white columnists who also had strong opinions. I was being too black; they were determined to guide me back to respectability.

In those environments, I knew if I wrote about race, many of my white colleagues would consider it unserious journalism. I also knew if I didn't, the subject would hardly ever get a sober examination in our pages other than after racially explosive events. At least that's the way it felt. For a long time, I spoke more about the years I spent being the region's primary real estate journalist, my reporting on the manufacturing industry, and my time as business editor than my writing and reporting on race. It was my subtle way of proving I was a legitimate journalist doing legitimate work despite my blackness.

At another paper, the white editor and publisher forbade me from comparing the Confederacy and its aftermath to the Holocaust. It would be unfair to white readers who revered the Confederate flag, I was told. All of this was happening as I was receiving "African heritage" letters and death and other kinds of threats I told almost no one about, and as I was struggling to balance the views of black people who had long been ignored and those of white readers who wanted to talk about race only if it was to tell black people that racial disparities were our own damn fault. I was also writing about my experiences of being a black man in the South who had never been racially profiled by police, which angered some of my black friends. I turned over one column to a Tea Party member so he could explain that group's point of view. I revealed my friendship with a white man who had decorated his house with the Confederate flag and *Gone with the Wind* memorabilia. I took to task civil rights icon Harry Belafonte when he referred to Colin Powell as essentially a house nigger, and I spoke of my bipartisan voting record. I even defended a local college professor who used the racial trope "go back to Africa" during an argument on campus. None of that convinced many white conservative readers, or a number of my white colleagues, that I was being fair to white people. All they wanted was for me to point out the flaws of black people or say nothing about race at all. Going beyond the parameters they set meant I was a black radical.

Many years after I left the paper, I asked some of my former colleagues what they thought of those incidents, particularly those concerning race in the newsroom. To a person, they hardly remembered any of them. Those incidents, which nearly convinced me to resign several times or quit the news industry altogether, hadn't registered with them at all. Not only that, my former publisher was offended because I asked the question at all, even though I was careful to couch my question with a sincere "I know it wasn't about racism for you, but..." She stopped returning my messages. I haven't spoken with her since.

NOTICING THE EMERGING STORY that would be the country's unprecedented shift in racial demographics, I organized an in-house race relations training session. It was designed to get journalists comfortable dealing with uncomfortable questions related to race. I believed then—and am absolutely convinced now—that such a change cannot come without major tension. Not all of it would be fueled by racism; much of it would be a fear born of the unknown. White people would be unnerved about the possibility of a United States in which they no longer made up the majority, just a plurality of the population. With massive change comes massive anxiety, even if the change is positive. That was my theory. That's why I thought it imperative that journalists get comfortable first before trying to tell that complex story.

The race relations sessions would take place over several weeks. I would lead a few and invite race relations experts I knew to lead others. During one of the first in which we were to speak uncomfortable truths and not judge one another based on them, a journalist of color blurted out why he "fucking hated white people." He didn't hate white people; he was just frustrated about and scarred by what he had been facing in an unkind South. A few of our white colleagues in the session were taken aback, offended. I felt it was a necessary part of the process. Tiptoeing around race or downplaying its explosiveness helped no one, particularly journalists. To me, it felt like a breakthrough. I was looking forward to going deeper. Then 9/11 happened and my editor canceled the rest of the sessions without telling me.

"We don't have to worry about that now," he later said. "Race no longer matters."

In Trumpland, time and again, I've found that many white people are quick to find reasons to back off from difficult conversations about race, no matter how dedicated they say they are to racial equality. It was no different inside the newsroom. As long as things remained calm and "civil"—and they determined what was or wasn't civil—they would engage, or at least pretend to. Dig beneath the surface and hit a few nerves, they quickly back off. I had no idea, though, that what nineteen terrorists did on that fateful Tuesday morning would provide them with yet another escape hatch.

I consider the decision to back off one of our great failures. We missed an opportunity to anticipate and understand the racial unrest I could see coming like a freight train. Many of my white colleagues thought I was "race-obsessed" because I could see what they couldn't and was trying to do something about it. They didn't realize that when it comes to race, when the shit begins rolling downhill, black people often smell it first. I knew the best chance to have difficult but fruitful conversations about race would be when they seemed unnecessary because we were feeling no immediate racial pain. In the middle of a racial storm, it's nearly impossible to reason with people across racial lines. In the Trump era, we are experiencing a racial storm unlike any we've experienced in my lifetime. It's overlaid with a hyper-partisanship that has infected every discussion, political and nonpolitical, supercharged by technology that daily blasts falsehoods to millions.

IT WAS THE TRIP TO GHANA that forced me to look anew at a United States that built monuments to honor the enslavers, not the enslaved, and what that said about racism and white supremacy in this country. In Ghana, I walked through a slave castle that included two Christian churches. A few centuries ago, Africans about to be sent into slavery an ocean away—if they were able to survive the horrific Middle Passage—were taught to worship a supposedly loving God who had sanctioned their enslavement before they exited through "The Door of No Return." I saw poverty-stricken black men and women praising a white Christian God introduced to them by men who had stolen black bodies. I listened to black men apologizing for the role their ancestors played in a slave trade that demonized, then profited, from dark skin like theirs.

I was there on a mission's trip with my church, a mostly black church founded by a black man who has been involved in the civil rights fight for decades, the Reverend Joe Washington. He believes it's vital that African-Americans take an active role in helping African countries. I went because Ghana is one of the West African countries from which I'm most likely descended, according to my family history and DNA results. I needed to see the place, touch the people. I led a journalism workshop for Ghanaian journalists, assisted a dentist who pulled rotting teeth, and explored impoverished areas that reminded me of scenes I experienced growing up in St. Stephen, South Carolina. It was my way of apologizing for having allowed white supremacy to color how I viewed the continent. I had allowed white supremacy to make me more ashamed of the enslaved than I was angry with the enslavers. I was ashamed of their dark skin, their kinky hair. I thought them weak and dumb, beneath me.

It was a surreal experience, the first time I could remember ever letting my racial guard down. I knew they knew I was more American than African, that I knew white supremacy had forever stamped their country, not just with the slave trade, but an untold number of foreign policy decisions made by U.S. presidents, including decisions by Richard Nixon, Ronald Reagan, and Trump. The year before I was born, during a phone call, Reagan referred to Africans as "monkeys" who are "still uncomfortable wearing shoes" and Nixon laughed heartily at the racist joke. When I was a grown man, Trump called such countries "shitholes." Still, in Ghana, race didn't matter because most everyone had dark skin like me.

I didn't have to wonder if the good or subpar service or side glances from strangers we received at restaurants, hotels, and in villages had anything to do with my skin color, which is always top of mind in South Carolina. Once, my wife and I struggled as we tried to determine why a white couple with whom we had agreed to share babysitting duties never let us watch their kids. We dropped our kids off at their place one night to go to dinner and a movie, a rare treat for a married couple with young kids. When we picked them up, we told them to call us to schedule their date. They didn't call. We called to remind them. They never called back. Was it because they didn't trust us with their white kids? If so, it would be the irony of ironies, given that older women in my wife's family and mine had sacrificed time with their children to care for white kids.

There was no way of knowing if that white couple's failure to return our calls had anything to do with race, at least not with certainty. They could have unexpectedly left town and not let us know, or maybe they were just overprotective the way some new parents are. But the question has never left me.

Being a black person in Trumpland, you face an endless string of such questions and almost never get a concrete answer. It's not like a lynching. But it threatens to slowly chip away at your sanity because you don't want to believe the worst, but know it's unwise to ignore the possibility. For two weeks, in Ghana, I felt my sanity begin to return. I still struggle with how best to guard it now that I'm back in Trumpland.

Guilty Even If Proven Innocent

EVERY TIME I THINK OF BRETT KAVANAUGH, I will think of Jamar Huggins.

Kavanaugh made it through one of the most contentious Senate confirmation hearings in recent memory to take a seat on the nation's highest court. Christine Blasey Ford alleged that Kavanaugh had sexually assaulted her when they were high school students. She couldn't pinpoint the house or the exact time or date—the alleged incident, after all, had occurred decades earlier—but she expressed no doubt it happened, and that it involved Kavanaugh and a friend at a party. She hadn't spoken about it publicly, though she had told a therapist and a few confidantes. She didn't want to but said she felt compelled to come forward when Kavanaugh was nominated for the Supreme Court.

During the Senate hearing, she was calm and collected. Kavanaugh fans said they were impressed. Then he took the stand. He let his teeth show and his anger

113

flow. His red-faced, spittle-flying, out-of-control rage that included repeating political conspiracy theories on live TV did not sink his chances; it was likely the reason he was confirmed. That and the anger displayed by my home state senator, Lindsey Graham. Each man was cheered by conservatives for using anger as a weapon. I don't know if that amounts to white privilege. I know it's not a privilege I have. It's why I spent many years avoiding writing the way I am in this book, afraid of white people's reaction to my black anger.

That's not why I will remember Jamar Huggins every time I see the name Brett Kavanaugh. It's because of an obscure 2016 case that made its way to the second-highest court in the land, the District of Columbia Court of Appeals. A Ph.D. student at the University of Virginia, Kathryn Sack, was trying to get data about the government's use of polygraphs for her dissertation. The Department of Defense denied her Freedom of Information Act request. She appealed. The case wound up before the DC circuit court, where Kavanaugh was a sitting judge. Kavanaugh, as part of a three-judge panel of the court, sided with DOD. But the why is more important than the what. He wrote that the government had proven there were legitimate law enforcement purposes for the polygraph results and other related information that had been compiled, and releasing them would "disclose techniques and procedures for law enforcement investigations" and possibly "risk circumvention of the law."

Kavanaugh wrote that the information should be exempt from FOIA requests because law enforcement agencies use it to test "the credibility of witnesses and criminal defendants" and "screen applicants for security clearances." Sack's requests, he said, "identify deficiencies in law enforcement agencies' polygraph programs" and could prove useful to criminal suspects "to subvert polygraph examinations."

He wrote those words even though the American Psychological Association said this years earlier:

> The accuracy (i.e., validity) of polygraph testing has long been controversial. An underlying problem is theoretical: There is no evidence that any pattern of physiological reactions is unique to deception. An honest person may be nervous when answering truthfully and a dishonest person may be non-anxious. Also, there are few good studies that validate the ability of polygraph procedures to detect deception. As Dr. Saxe and Israeli psychologist Gershon Ben-Shahar (1999) note, "it may, in fact, be impossible to conduct a proper validity study." In real-world situations, it's very difficult to know what the truth is.

Still, there are plenty of constitutional experts who would side with Kavanaugh on technical legal grounds. I'm not here to discuss the finer points of the law, but rather their practical effects. When you cut through the legalese, Kavanaugh believed the government had successfully demonstrated that the polygraph could be effective and should be protected as an investigative tool, even if an imperfect one. His tune changed when talk turned to the possibility of his taking one during his confirmation hearing. When Democratic Senator Kamala Harris asked if he would submit to the "lie detector," Kavanaugh quickly said the test was "not reliable." Republican Senator Chuck Grassley essentially declared the same when talk turned to whether the results of a polygraph Blasey Ford had taken—which showed that she was not being deceitful, according to the test's criteria—should be officially entered into the record.

Heads Kavanaugh wins, tails Kavanaugh can't lose.

The public is repeatedly told polygraph results are not admissible in criminal cases. Again, on technical, legal grounds, that's true in most states in most situations. The deeper reality, lived far away from privileged men and women in black robes debating the finer points of constitutional law, is that if you are a Jamar Huggins rather than a Brett Kavanaugh, it's heads you lose and tails you get sent to prison anyway.

Huggins voluntarily took the test after being fingered for armed home invasion. The "inconclusive" or "failed" result convinced prosecutors to charge him with felonies that eventually resulted in a fifteen-year prison sentence. After he had been convicted, a similar result on yet another test convinced prosecutors to fight his appeal for a second trial. Each of those decisions was made not in the courtroom but in the prosecutor's office. In the eyes of those who make and interpret our laws, "good" results from a polygraph are not enough to establish the credibility of a woman who said she was nearly raped. In their eyes, it should not even be considered if the reputation of a powerful white man is at stake.

In the eyes of those who carry out laws, a "bad" result on a polygraph is enough to send a black man to prison and keep him there. The unethical use of the polygraph was only part of the injustice inflicted upon Huggins and his family.

I POLITELY LISTENED as Dinedra Smith told me her brother, Jamar Huggins, had been unfairly prosecuted. We were in a conference room in the *Sun News* building with Kia Gagum, Huggins's girlfriend. They told me about an armed home invasion in Conway, provided copies of court and police documents, and detailed the ways they believed his case had gone wrong. At the end of that hour-long conversation, I thanked them and said I might take a look. But I wasn't really interested. I was tired. Tired of writing about race and crime and discrimination, tired of examining an unjust system its most loyal supporters say is the best in the world.

I didn't begin investigating the case until I received an official transcript of the trial. That's how I learned that a young girl named Mariah Eckler buried her head under a blanket and covered her ears to drown out the fear she heard in her mother's voice, which came in scattered words and screams from another room. It was about two a.m., five days before Christmas in 2012. The twelve-year-old was experiencing an event she's likely never to forget in a house on a dead-end road called Memory Lane, usually so calm that unlocked front doors in the neighborhood were common.

Her ordeal would become an example of just how difficult it is to define one of the most relied-upon yet least understood legal principles in America's criminal justice system. But it wouldn't be her ordeal alone. Willie Dean Whaley, who was ninety years old the night of the crime, suffered, too. She had been reliant upon her grandson, Huggins, for round-the-clock care for at least two years.

"Ain't no way Jamar is guilty," she said.

Just what constitutes guilt beyond a reasonable doubt? In this case, there was no hard evidence, the primary witness and a detective admitted lying, the judge considered dismissing the charges, the prosecution and defense scrambled to change strategies midstream—and still the jury handed down a verdict that baffled even an alternate juror.

"What exactly is proof 'beyond a reasonable doubt'? Anyone who has served as a criminal juror knows that the rule is not easy to understand. There is always some possible uncertainty about the case. Exactly what kind of uncertainty counts as a legal 'doubt'? Exactly when are legal 'doubts' about the guilt of the accused 'reasonable'?"

James Q. Whitman of Yale Law School pondered this in *The Origins of Reasonable Doubt*. "Even some of the most sophisticated members of the legal profession find the question too difficult to answer. The result is troubling indeed. Once a jury has determined a person to be guilty 'beyond a reasonable doubt,' that person's fate is almost always sealed."

I was a juror twice, witnessed several trials as a journalist, and have consulted with prosecutors, defense attorneys, legal analysts, and judges and justices on the issue. I still can't tell you what *reasonable doubt* means, other than it is whatever a jury decides. In a DUI case, we were told the defendant's blood alcohol level was above the legal limit. I did not know that didn't make it an open-and-shut legal case. The judge told us we could decide that that fact, alone, was enough to declare guilt. Or we could take other factors into account. *Above the legal limit* didn't mean what the words plainly suggest it does.

We also had the testimony of the well-decorated veteran state trooper who had pulled the driver over that night. The car was being driven erratically, he told us from the witness stand. I did not doubt a word he said, he was so sure and clinical and articulate. But when the prosecutor popped in the dashcam video, to underscore the claims the trooper had made, we saw no evidence of erratic driving. All we saw was a silver sedan whose left back tire slightly touched the yellow centerline on the road maybe once over the course of a mile or so. The defense provided proof that the defendant had been taking medication for an ear infection earlier and had consumed "a few beers." That was the sum total of evidence we were provided.

From that, we were supposed to decide the fate of the man, a white Philadelphia cop who was visiting Myrtle Beach for a week's vacation. Should he potentially serve a few years or several months in prison or on probation? Or should he keep his badge and pension? At the outset of deliberations, a couple of the jurors insisted that only the results of the blood alcohol test mattered; they demanded a guilty verdict. Others considered the medication excuse. I was most moved by the huge discrepancy between what the trooper said and what the video showed. I voted not guilty. The man and his wife hugged and cried after hearing the rest of the jury did as well.

And yet, I don't know if I did the right thing, because I'm still not sure what the right thing is or was supposed to be. Relying solely upon the results of a blood alcohol test in a DUI case was reasonable. But it is also reasonable to consider other factors. The man was on medication. He was not driving dangerously. The trooper had not been honest, or at least not accurate. Which of us was right? Any of us? A bevy of research suggests a not guilty verdict in a case like that, or any criminal case, is less likely when the defendant is black. Would a black man have gotten the same kind of serious deliberation we gave that white Philadelphia cop? How can we ever be sure? How sure must we be before ruining a person's life? Or withholding justice from a victim?

What's worse is that the reasonable doubt standard was not built on a solid legal foundation.

"Convicting an innocent defendant was regarded...as a potential mortal sin," Whitman wrote. "The reasonable doubt rule developed in response to this disquieting possibility. It was originally a theological doctrine, intended to reassure jurors that they could convict the defendant without risking their own salvation."

Neuroscientific research suggests there is folly in trying to determine a single "reasonable" standard. The race of the defendant and victim, the racial makeup of the jury, the camera angle of videos shown during a trial, the influence of police lineups, and a host of other factors color how an individual juror decides between guilty and not guilty, even when the juror is trying to be objective. Subtle phrasing of sentences, how a defendant is dressed, and his mannerisms also impact trial outcomes. Not only that, though we believe our brains record memories like video cameras, they don't. Our emotions and trauma affect how we store the images that become memories, and not always accurately. The brain essentially has to piece those images together later to come up with what we believe are our memories, and those are the accounts eyewitnesses convey to a jury from the witness stand. It's also why, oddly, both Blasey Ford and Kavanaugh could have been telling the truth. If the attempted rape happened, it stands to reason Blasey Ford's brain would have been the one more likely to store images of the incident, because it deeply affected her, while Kavanaugh might genuinely not remember or might have trouble retrieving the images.

We also know that race affects our memories and perceptions, particularly when dealing with someone not of the same race. We are often wrong because we wrongly believe our wanting to be right is enough to make us right. We fool ourselves into thinking we are purely objective beings when there really is no such thing. Brain processes and the environment in which we spend most of our time affect everything we do, say, and believe, as well as a mix of other genetic factors we still don't fully understand.

"Jurors and judges can't help but be influenced by their backgrounds and experiences. The laws and facts are filtered through the lens of our identities," Adam Benforado, author of *Unfair: The New Science of Criminal Injustice*, told me. "Even when juries are given guidance as to the meaning of 'beyond a reasonable doubt,' we can't ensure the consistency in application that we promise…It appears that some of the worst racial bias in our system occurs because of implicit biases that operate beyond people's conscious awareness or control."

During deliberations, the strength of a lone juror's personality may end up being more important than the evidence being weighed. That's why I was surprised when prosecutors didn't object when defense attorneys cleared me to sit on a jury. They knew about my strong critiques of the criminal justice system—a prosecutor once tried to get me thrown out of a courtroom because of my columns; though the judge declined to—which suggested that I was unlikely to sit quietly in a jury room and accept what others thought. I didn't. In those mini-experiments, I voted not guilty in one case, guilty in another. What does that say about me? There was real disagreement in the DUI case before we landed on not guilty, none in the other case, which involved another nonfatal driving incident. I know the verdicts hinged as much on the makeup of the jury as on the quality of the evidence, and maybe more.

It's why millions of Americans were convinced that the verdict in the high-profile O. J. Simpson murder case was reasonable—while millions of others thought it was a travesty. The revelation that a primary detective in the case was known for using the word *nigger* and bragging about routinely violating the constitutional rights of defendants, coupled with the mishandling of key evidence, was enough to justify a not guilty verdict even if they strongly suspected Simpson had murdered two people, some believed, and still do. Others thought such factors were not enough to override what they saw as overwhelming evidence of guilt, as well as a lack of plausible alternatives. Each side is convinced it reached its final judgment based on a reasonable analysis of the facts. Which conclusion was most reasonable in the legal sense? Only the jury's—no matter how they arrived at it.

"All this means that it is no surprise that our law finds itself in a state of confusion today," Whitman wrote. "We are asking the reasonable doubt standard to serve a function that it was not originally designed to serve."

A FEW HOURS BEFORE Mariah Eckler's ordeal began, the twelve-year-old had helped her mother, Angela Eckler, set up a Christmas tree and decorations bought as a surprise by a family friend. The pair then cuddled together on the bed to watch *Elf*, a movie about the surreal experience of a toddler accidentally taken to the North Pole and raised as one of Santa's helpers. Instead of being involved in a silly fantasy like the Will Ferrell character, Mariah Eckler soon found herself in the middle of an ugly reality.

Two men, one in a dark mask and dark gloves, rushed through the front door of her home and put her mother in a chokehold so tight that bruises on her neck would last for weeks. They dragged her by the hair through a living room whose darkness was broken only by glare from the TV and tea lights in the window. Angela Eckler was hurled into the side of her grandfather's rocking chair before one of the men stuck a gun in her face demanding "the fucking money."

A woman who accompanied the men to the house that night, DeAungela "Shante" Montgomery, would tell a detective that Huggins was one of those men. That's why about a month after the break-in, Huggins was charged with first-degree burglary, armed robbery, and kidnapping. He went to trial almost two years later. Including jury selection, it lasted three days. Neither of the Ecklers could identify the men who attacked them, there was no hard evidence linking Huggins to the crime—and the main witness, Montgomery, had told multiple, contradictory versions of the same story—but by the end of the trial, there was no reasonable doubt he was involved, at least in the minds of twelve jurors, the prosecutor, the judge, the police detective who investigated the case, and the victims.

After the verdict, a portion of a victim impact statement by Mariah Eckler was read aloud in the courtroom by the prosecutor before Judge Benjamin H. Culbertson handed down a sentence.

"I saw a man with a gun, Jamar Huggins, then the other guy that was with him ask me, 'Where's the money?'" the statement read, even though she had not been able to identify the man with the gun—because he was wearing a mask—and only mentioned Huggins's name because of what the prosecutor and police told her and the jury. "I thought for sure Jamar was going to shoot my mom."

Culbertson sentenced Huggins to concurrent fifteen- and ten-year prison sentences for first-degree burglary, armed robbery, and kidnapping. But given that it was dark, the man with the gun wore a mask, and the entire case against Huggins hinged solely on the credibility of a woman who was addicted to crack cocaine, from where did such certainty come?

ABOUT A WEEK BEFORE the home invasion at the Ecklers', Adrian Moore was wandering a stretch of Church Street in Conway that police know as a place addicts go to get drugs. Someone called 911 to report a man's "bizarre" behavior. "I'll kill myself," he was yelling.

Emergency officials picked Moore up near the corner of Racepath Avenue and Wright Boulevard and took him to Conway Medical Center. He would spend the next few weeks there, mostly under suicide watch. He was admitted about a week before Angela and Mariah Eckler stared down the barrel of a small black gun being held by a strange man in their home.

As part of his investigation into the Eckler home invasion, Horry County Police Detective Jonathan Martin visited Moore in the hospital. The conversation was recorded, and it included this exchange:

"Your fiancée...[was] the victim of a home invasion," Martin told Moore. "Some guys broke in, looking for you...beat her up a little bit."

"What?" Moore returned. "When was this?"

"She's a little shook up, you can imagine," Martin said. "They haven't stayed in the house since; their Christmas has pretty much been ruined."

"Did they hit her?"

"They held the twelve-year-old at gunpoint asking where the money was."

Moore told Martin he had been buying and selling cocaine, including a "quarter" from an associate he only knew as "T." He admitted making ATM withdrawals from the account he shared with Angela Eckler, his then live-in fiancée. Moore had used the money to "hustle" and buy four hundred dollars' worth of cocaine he planned to sell for eight hundred, as well as "drinks and things like that" during the days he told Eckler he had been working as a day laborer. One of his drug suppliers was a man he only knew as "Juice," whom he believed was the man who visited Eckler's home the afternoon of the home invasion.

"Who would want money from you?" Martin asked.

"I didn't owe money to anyone," Moore said.

"You know any pretty black females?" Martin asked, in reference to the description Eckler provided of the woman who knocked on the front door at the start of the home invasion.

Moore guessed it could have been a woman he did drugs with, whom he knew as "Sharmaine." That woman, who was later revealed to be Montgomery, "and people that she knew" sold drugs for Moore, he said.

Montgomery "has some debts," Moore told Martin, "so they must think I have some debts because I was with her."

Moore's revelations led Martin to Montgomery, who eventually told the detective the many ways she had become consumed by a drug addiction, in part to explain how she became involved with the men who broke into the Eckler home. She recounted a particularly bad night, when she anxiously shook twenty dollars of drugs into a crack pipe after rushing home with her buy.

"I started smoking with the door wide open," she told Detective Martin less than a month after the Ecklers were attacked.

On another day, she had awakened to find her four-year-old lying next to her on the bed, afraid it wouldn't be much longer before she passed out in front of her daughter. There were even darker times after she began going on crack cocaine binges with Moore, who was by then Angela Eckler's fiancé.

"I just realized I got a habit, like a bad addiction," she said. "I got tired of it. I was just sick of being high."

She was saying this in an interview room at J. Reuben Long Detention Center, where she was being held for her alleged role in an armed robbery that happened a week after the Eckler home invasion. In that case, Montgomery had been charged with accessory before the fact of a felony, two counts of armed robbery, two counts of kidnapping, and first-degree burglary. A man had given her a ride and was waiting on Singleton Street at her request, according to a Conway police report. Montgomery and a gun-wielding man allegedly stole six dollars and a phone.

Her interrogation was recorded. When asked about the Eckler case, Montgomery initially denied knowing anything. "To be honest, I used to do drugs and I really do not know," she said. But during her winding, contradictory statement, Montgomery mentioned Huggins. It was the first time his name was connected to the case. An earlier check of phone records by Martin had turned up no contact between Huggins and Moore, the presumed target of the home invasion. The jury would not be told that detail, nor would it know that Moore never mentioned Huggins, or about other inconsistencies apparent in Montgomery's statements.

During the interrogation, Martin showed Montgomery a photo of Moore. At first she said she didn't recognize the face, then blurted out, "Drake," Moore's street name. She only hung out with him once, no twice, she quickly corrected herself, a three-day stay at a Conway hotel and later at her house. Moore had a really bad habit, would act strangely and needed someone with him when he did drugs, she said.

"He had a lot of money and stuff. He had a *lot* of money."

"Have you ever been to Drake's house?" Martin asked.

Just once, she said, when Moore sneaked her into a back room. He would walk out and talk to Eckler, walk back into the room and smoke crack with Montgomery, and repeat the process. Martin pulled out a sheet with photos of a lineup of six women. Montgomery's picture, No. 3, was circled.

"This is the lady who robbed me," a note on it read. It was initialed "AE" in cursive.

"Either she seen the wrong girl...," Montgomery said.

The note wasn't from Eckler, who hadn't been able to identify Montgomery at that point. It was written by Martin as a ruse—a fact that would later confuse Montgomery when she testified during the Huggins trial. The detective didn't do anything legally improper by implying she'd been identified. The Supreme Court has ruled that police officers can lie to trick suspects into revealing information they otherwise wouldn't.

"You didn't go one time and knock on the door looking for Drake?"

"No," Montgomery said.

"Okay, I'm not gonna play around; we don't got time," Martin said.

Then he told her about the home invasion, how a young woman knocked on Eckler's door and two men rushed in behind her.

"I have a lawyer and I don't wanna talk no more," Montgomery said. "Because this is a bit confu[sing]."

Had the interrogation stopped there, Huggins likely wouldn't be in a Columbia, South Carolina, prison serving fifteen years. But it didn't stop, which raises constitutional questions. Martin did not read her the Miranda warning after Montgomery asked for a lawyer, an issue that could have been raised in Montgomery's trial had she not taken a plea agreement to settle multiple charges in two cases.

"That's fine," Martin responded. "I'm gonna go get the warrants right now. It's gonna be armed robbery times two and kidnapping times two. Okay?"

"Okay, because I don't know what is going on," Montgomery said. "I honestly don't know what's going on."

"That's fine, I was giving you a chance to say what you wanted to say because maybe you weren't involved with it to the point that you didn't know what was gonna happen. Maybe you were made to do it, but that's fine."

"And so, if I talk...," Montgomery asked.

"That's up to you," Martin continued.

"Okay, I'm gonna just be honest," Montgomery said.

Martin, along with another detective, sat back down. The conversation that would change Huggins's life was about to begin.

ACCORDING TO MONTGOMERY, the state's only witness against Huggins, this is how Mariah and Angela Eckler came to be held at gunpoint in their home a few days before Christmas in 2012. Huggins showed up at Montgomery's house the night of December 20 cursing, threatening to hurt her if she didn't help him find Moore, who had allegedly borrowed drugs from him "on credit." She felt obligated to get into Huggins's dark blue Cadillac and lead him to a house on Memory Lane that Moore had been sharing with Angela Eckler, his then fiancée.

Huggins wore a mask and pointed a gun in the face of Eckler and her twelve-year-old daughter, Montgomery said. He was one of the men who dragged Angela Eckler through the house and was yelling, "Where's the fucking money?"

The two men eventually forced the Ecklers into a bathroom before rummaging through Moore's belongings and stealing Mariah Eckler's birthday money—fifteen dollars—and video games.

Montgomery was specific in this version of her confession; after initially denying everything, she supplied a cell phone number and directions to Huggins's home. She'd later say she knew what Huggins looked like because she saw him through a hotel window as Huggins and Moore allegedly conducted a drug transaction.

"I just didn't want to be a part of it," Montgomery said. "Had he not had a gun and I didn't smoke [the drugs], I would have called the police on him."

Montgomery said the two men pushed her aside as they forced their way into the house. She ran back to the car and was only vaguely aware of what was going to happen, she told Martin.

"When this man [Huggins] come to my house and I know his reputation, he is dangerous," Montgomery went on. "He don't care about punching you in the face, taking his gun and pistol-whipping you. He don't care what kind of person you is. If you owe him something, he want it. I just know he is that determined to get it. If I had a' known he was going to run in there and do all of that, I would've just took the knockout in my face."

But that wasn't her only version of the events, and not everything she said matched up with what Moore had told the detective. Montgomery claimed she came to know what Huggins looked like by peeking out of a hotel window—but Huggins would later say that though they didn't know each other well, she had performed oral sex on him once. He also once angrily told Montgomery he didn't want to have much else to do "with no crackhead," according to his sister.

Montgomery also said she had only "hung out with" Moore a few times—but Moore said Montgomery helped him sell drugs.

Montgomery initially said she and Moore only bought drugs from another dealer, a man she knew as "Juice." Montgomery later said she saw Moore receive drugs from Huggins.

During the initial interrogation, Montgomery said she was pushed violently out of the way when the men rushed into the house, and that she did not know they would be robbing those inside. In a later statement, Montgomery said she ran back to the car because she thought Eckler's barking dog was attacking the two men.

Under oath during the Huggins trial, her story changed again, to this: "[W]hen I first knocked on the door [Angela Eckler] didn't open her screen door. She opened her first door, and after I asked for [Moore] she say he wasn't there. So I turned around and walked off. When I walked off, she opened her screen door and was hollering at me, trying to make me stop so she could tell me where he was at, but I kept on walking and got back inside the vehicle . . . I knew what was going to happen . . . that she was going to be robbed."

On the stand, Montgomery identified a man she said helped plan the home invasion—a man she had been involved with in an unrelated robbery. During the initial interrogation, Montgomery described Huggins as five feet six or seven inches tall and 280 pounds with long dreadlocks and a "grill" (jewelry for the teeth, usually gold or silver) in his mouth.

Huggins did have dreadlocks and once had a "grill," but he had discarded the tooth jewelry well before the

Ecklers were robbed. After further questioning by Martin, she said Huggins weighed "up to two hundred pounds."

Huggins is five feet six inches tall and weighed about 150 pounds.

During the initial interrogation, Montgomery told Martin she was afraid of Huggins. But during a subsequent recorded telephone conversation while she was in jail, Montgomery expressed no fear of the man she called the "boy with the gun." She said that man—she did not say who he was—was being "a pussy about" the robbery and should just shut up.

Moore, the alleged target of the home invasion at his fiancée's home, told Detective Martin that Montgomery owed money to drug dealers who may have targeted him because of his relationship with her. Montgomery told Martin the opposite—that it was Moore who owed money.

None of these inconsistencies would be explored during the trial. Nevertheless, Martin used Montgomery's confession to seek an arrest warrant for Huggins. A judge granted it.

A few days later, two U.S. marshals showed up at the home where Huggins was taking care of his ailing ninety-year-old grandmother and took him to J. Reuben Long Detention Center, a jail named after the grandfather of the man who would defend Huggins in court.

BY THE TIME the case reached a courtroom almost two years after the crime, Huggins had repeatedly denied any involvement even though Detective Martin used the same "police deception" with Huggins that he had used to persuade Montgomery to confess. Martin pretended to have more evidence than he did. He produced a photo of Moore. Huggins quickly said he had never seen Moore and didn't know who he was—the kind of clear-cut denial that would have been damaging had any connection between Huggins and Moore been unearthed later, but no such evidence ever was uncovered.

"I just want you to please don't just look at me as, 'Okay, I got this case closed, this a criminal,'" Huggins pleaded with Martin. "No, man. Please?! Sometimes you have innocent people who get jammed up in situations."

Martin told him he had the right man, that he knew Huggins was guilty. Huggins admitted he had gotten into trouble when he was younger and that he got into fights and still smoked pot occasionally, but insisted he hadn't touched hard drugs, like cocaine, in almost a decade. He had been shot before, a close friend had recently been murdered, and other friends were serving long prison sentences. Those hard street realities had convinced him to change, he told Martin.

He was the primary caretaker of a ninety-year-old grandmother who suffers from a variety of ailments, a woman who coughs "all night" and "calls my name for me to come in there and bring her some water" or call 911. He had been doing that around the clock for at least two years by that point, a fact his mother and sisters confirmed, and was about to land a job with Walmart before he was arrested.

"I just hope you do some more investigating because I ain't had nothing to do with this; real talk," Huggins told Martin. "You can check my background and my record … I'm locked up for something I ain't had nothing to do with."

Martin never told Huggins when or where the break-in occurred. Instead, Martin withheld that information while telling Huggins things that weren't true, hoping to trip up Huggins into a confession or something that could be used against him during the trial. Huggins speculated it could have happened late one night when Montgomery and an acquaintance of theirs borrowed his car and brought it back a short while later "looking all strange." He thought they used the car to have sex.

Huggins's mother, Helen Huggins, said she knew where her son was that night—in his room, in bed. After a late night at a Conway Bingo parlor a couple of miles away, she and a friend, Jennette Scott, returned home and momentarily disturbed his sleep. Her son didn't leave the house until several hours later, she said.

"We already knew that girl was lying because we saw [Jamar] that night," Scott told me.

Martin never asked either of them about Huggins's whereabouts. Horry County Police Chief Saundra Rhodes said it wasn't Martin's responsibility to ask about an alibi. If she had been Huggins's mother and had that kind of information, she would have made sure everyone knew, Rhodes said.

But because Martin used "police deception" during his interrogation of Huggins, there was initial confusion about which night, making it difficult to pin down a reliable alibi.

"I told the marshals and I told the people at the courthouse, but nobody would listen," Helen Huggins said.

She never spoke with her son's attorney, John Long, though, and it's not clear why. Long didn't want to comment on the record. The jury would know none of this when they met to consider Montgomery's testimony. Helen Huggins and Scott wouldn't be called during the three-day trial.

Neither would jurors know that Huggins had turned down multiple plea deals over the course of two years— including one that would have freed him almost immediately—believing it was important to "send the right message to his two children," his sister Dinedra Smith said.

"He wasn't going to say he did something he didn't do," she said.

During the trial, the prosecution's star witness unexpectedly gave Huggins and his family hope the jury would also believe he was innocent.

SOLICITOR DONNA ELDER called Montgomery to the stand. Montgomery had already pleaded guilty to her role in the crime, and to another armed robbery that happened seven days later.

Elder had little choice in calling Montgomery first. There was no DNA evidence, no eyewitness evidence, no phone records—nothing else connecting Huggins to the case. Montgomery's statement during questioning was the reason Detective Martin had secured an arrest warrant for Huggins. The beyond-a-reasonable-doubt standard rested solely on her word.

Elder began by having Montgomery tell the jury she was serving a ten-year sentence for her role in two armed robberies—the maximum penalty was thirty years each—and that she had received no help from the solicitor's office in exchange for her testimony, according to the court transcript of the trial.

"One of the armed robberies that you have been convicted for, I want to take you back to the one in December of 2012," Elder said. "Do you remember that?"

"Yes, ma'am," Montgomery answered.

"Okay. Do you remember going to a house on Memory Lane?"

"Yes, ma'am."

"And tell me about what happened when you went to that house."

"I can't really remember."

"All right. Do you remember giving statements before?"

"No. I'm on medication now. So, I don't...I can't remember nothing really."

After a little prompting, Montgomery said she remembered telling a detective that she and two men robbed the Ecklers—but that Huggins was not with them.

"Do you remember telling [the detective] that it was Junk?" Elder asked, using Huggins's nickname. (Montgomery and police struggled to keep the nicknames of Huggins and the men allegedly involved in the home invasion straight, and there was a dispute about which man was commonly known as "Junk" and which one was "Juice.")

"Yeah. I remember the name...but [Huggins] doesn't look like the same person," Montgomery answered.

Elder pressed, pushing Montgomery to say she told police Huggins was involved. She reminded Montgomery that she had described the color of the car, had told the detective where he lived, and that he had on a mask and was armed with a handgun.

"Most of what I said to the detective was not true because—" Montgomery said before Elder cut her off.

"Okay. What about yesterday?" Elder tried to get Montgomery to say she repeated her claim a day before the trial.

"I don't even...to tell you the truth I don't...I can only say who went with me. That's all I can say. I really can't even recall that night."

"But you pled guilty to it?"

"Yes. I pled guilty to it. I was convinced that that was the only deal that I was going to get and if I brought it to trial, I can get up to thirty years. So, I took the ten."

The testimony Elder was hoping for—Montgomery pointing out Huggins from the stand—instead became a heated back-and-forth that included more inconsistencies, with Montgomery repeatedly saying Huggins was not involved.

"I told them [Huggins], but it was a lie," Montgomery said. "We...I didn't want to say the name that we got [drugs] from, and I still don't want to say the name."

John Long, Huggins's lawyer, had readied a defense that would question Montgomery's reliability as a witness, given her crack cocaine addiction, maybe point out the holes in her story. After she recanted on the stand, Long settled on one question.

"Ms. Montgomery, this is not the person who went in that home invasion with you, is it?" he asked, referring to Huggins.

"No, sir."

"It is not the person who went in the home invasion with you?" Long repeated for emphasis.

"No, sir."

"That's all the questions I have."

In a world in which the beyond-a-reasonable-doubt standard made sense and was well defined, there would have been no reason for Long to have asked Montgomery anything else. He knew that with her recantation on the stand, the prosecution had no actual evidence showing Huggins was involved in the home invasion, literally nothing. The prosecution didn't have bad evidence or questionable evidence—at that point, they had none, which was less than the evidence they had been relying upon for two years, the word of a crack-addicted woman who had been known to lie from the beginning of the investigation.

Long's decision, to essentially guarantee jury members would not be confused by legalese as he and the prosecutor went back and forth debating the finer points of the law, made perfect sense in a world that makes perfect sense. They heard the prosecutor's main witness say the defendant was not involved. In a world in which *beyond a reasonable doubt* meant what the words suggest they do, nothing else should have been necessary to guarantee Huggins's freedom. But that perfect world is not the U.S. criminal justice system, for in that world, the real one, Prosecutor Elder didn't turn to the judge with bowed head and say she no longer had a case and that the charges should be dismissed, but without prejudice, in case investigators later uncovered real evidence linking Huggins to the crime. Instead, Elder tried again to get Montgomery to say Huggins was involved, but Montgomery kept on insisting Huggins was not there that night.

During a break for the jury, Judge Benjamin Culbertson said he knew Elder's case relied upon Montgomery's testimony and that a directed verdict—which would have freed Huggins no matter what the jury was thinking—was a close call. Judges are reluctant to stop a trial, even though a directed verdict is allowed when the prosecution has not presented enough evidence for a jury to be able to reasonably come to a guilty verdict. Montgomery's initial statement was enough to meet that standard, if only barely, Culbertson ruled. Legalese. *Heads, Huggins loses, tails, Huggins is convicted anyway.*

Had Culbertson declared the evidence was too weak, Montgomery's recanting on the stand would have been as pivotal as the moments dramatized in criminal justice shows such as *Law & Order*. Because Culbertson decided not to, the inconsistent story Montgomery told before trial went unexamined. Elder then called the victim, Angela Eckler, to the stand. She confirmed that she couldn't identify the men and didn't see the car they drove. Elder called Detective Martin to testify, who confirmed the only reason the investigation turned to Huggins was the initial statement from Montgomery.

On cross-examination, Long, Huggins's attorney, hammered Martin about the lies he told to further the case. Martin explained why a police officer's lies were sometimes necessary and have been justified by the Supreme Court. Earlier in the trial, those lies had confused Montgomery, causing her to mistakenly believe Martin had presented her with a lineup photo that already had Huggins's mugshot circled. On the stand, Montgomery believed the lineup photo she had been shown was of Huggins and other male suspects, but it was actually one that included Montgomery's own mugshot among other women as he tried to trick her into confessing.

Long also pushed Martin about the decision to rely upon Montgomery's word, knowing she was addicted to crack cocaine. The detective claimed he didn't know Montgomery was a "crackhead."

"Mr. Long wants you to believe that you can't believe anything [Montgomery] says because he called her an addicted crackhead," Elder argued during closing arguments. "There is absolutely no evidence, nothing, that she was an addict or that she was a crackhead...To label her as an addicted crackhead without any evidence to support that is just...not appropriate."

Elder's argument was flatly untrue. She had to know it if she had spent any time listening to the interrogation audio. There was extensive evidence of Montgomery's severe crack cocaine addiction. That evidence was not presented to the jury. When Montgomery recanted her original statement, Long felt there was no reason to try to impeach her credibility. During the initial interrogation, Montgomery told Detective Martin she was ashamed of having traded sex to pay off debts for drugs, how she was afraid her behavior was spiraling out of control and could eventually affect her two young children. She told him she ignored her family when they tried an intervention, how she was scheduled to go into long-term rehab to reclaim her life, how her arrest short-circuited those plans. (I later confirmed that an activist couple who have helped many people in the area were in the process of helping Montgomery get clean before she was arrested.)

During closing arguments, Elder then suggested Montgomery recanted on the stand because she was afraid—though offered no evidence for that theory either.

"Don't you think she ha[d] all the incentive and motivation in January of 2013 when she identified Jamar Huggins to tell the truth," Elder asked the jury, "when it was fresh in her mind to tell the truth, because lying was certainly not going to help her and lying to a police officer about a felony would have resulted in even more charges?"

Long countered that Elder's argument was baseless speculation and reminded the jury that the prosecution's star witness said Huggins was not involved in the home invasion.

"He comes into this courtroom…wearing a cloak of innocence," Long said. "For him to be proven guilty, the State has to take off that robe of innocence, prove him guilty beyond a reasonable doubt of each and every element of each and every crime…The testimony you heard can't get you there from here."

The jury, Judge Culbertson said, was to consider "only the testimony which has been presented from the witness stand, any exhibits which have been made a part of the record in this case and any stipulations of counsel."

They could believe all or part of a witness's testimony, as well as a witness's bias or credibility. With that, the jury filed out of the courtroom and began deliberations.

THE JURY WAS TASKED with a decision that could, in the harshest scenario, lead to the then thirty-two-year-old Huggins being in prison until he was more than a hundred years old. A guilty verdict would guarantee at least a fifteen-year sentence because of mandatory minimums in South Carolina. They did not examine fingerprints, eyewitness accounts from the victims, or results from the touch DNA swabs linking Huggins to the crime—because there was no such evidence. They did not consider phone or text messages connecting Huggins to the man police said was the real target of the home invasion— because there were none. For a variety of technical legal reasons, strategy chosen by the prosecution and defense, and rulings by Judge Culbertson, the jury wouldn't know that Huggins always maintained his innocence. He turned down several plea offers that would have set him free before court. (In the United States, more than 90 percent of criminal cases end in plea agreements, providing a defendant a shorter sentence but also forever branding him a convicted felon. That was true in Horry County as well.)

During a phone call from the J. Reuben Long Detention Center when he didn't know he was being recorded, Huggins said Montgomery and a man he knew may have done something and "got his name in it" when they borrowed his car late one night, the same thing he alluded to during an interrogation—another fact the jury wouldn't hear. Neither would they know of an alibi corroborated by Huggins's mother and a family friend.

The jury's decision would rest upon one thing— Montgomery's word. And they hadn't even been equipped with a complete view of that.

While testimony revealed that Montgomery had been involved in another armed robbery, neither the prosecution nor the defense explained to the jury that crime was seven days after the home invasion and that she pleaded guilty to luring a man to be robbed by one of the initial suspects in the home invasion. Her codefendant in that case was Christopher Jamal Montgomery, who was also charged with three counts of kidnapping, four counts of armed robbery, and four counts of possession of a weapon during a violent crime when he was accused of pistol-whipping and robbing a disabled man at a Myrtle Beach motel a couple of hours before the Eckler home invasion in Conway. He allegedly stole $190, a digital camera, and a cell phone during the armed robbery of a man and woman five days earlier.

Because the prosecution and detective claimed to not know about Montgomery's significant drug problem, the jury had been led to believe she had used the drug but—as Elder erroneously said during closing arguments—there was "absolutely no evidence" she was a crack addict. The jury also didn't know the extent of the inconsistencies in Montgomery's initial statement, the one that led to Huggins's prosecution and convinced Culbertson to hand the case to the jury. All the jury knew was that the woman who on the stand told them Huggins was not involved had previously said he was.

On that amount of information, they were told to make a judgment that would forever alter Huggins's life in an effort to bring justice to a mother and daughter who had been victimized in their own home. According to the principals involved in this and other criminal cases—law enforcement officials, defense attorneys, prosecutors, judges, legal analysts—that's how the system is supposed to work. It was not an accident the jury was asked to decide based on almost no evidence; it was by design.

After about two hours of deliberations, the jury asked Judge Culbertson a single question. "We want to know the first date the investigator Martin interviewed Ms. Montgomery." The jurors were told: January 11, 2013, at 9:41 a.m., about three weeks after the crime.

A little less than two hours later, the jury reached a verdict. "Guilty."

Culbertson thanked then dismissed them before listening to a statement from Huggins's ninety-year-old grandmother, who pleaded for leniency and said she knew Huggins was innocent, and a letter written by fourteen-year-old Mariah Eckler, who urged the judge to give Huggins the maximum.

Elder tried to present what she said was a failed polygraph test by Huggins but admitted that had the results been different she would not have accepted it as proving his innocence. Culbertson disregarded it. Huggins's lawyer once again asked Culbertson to intervene. "There is absolutely no evidence for the jury to base their conviction upon," Long argued.

Culbertson agreed "one hundred percent" that it was "a close call" and that an appeals court might determine that he had committed a legal error. "I go with the jury's verdict and…they just believed Ms. Montgomery's prior statement and didn't believe her testimony at trial," Culbertson said while denying Long's motion. "All I do is look to see if there is any evidence in the record, and then it's up to the jury to draw the conclusions they want to draw."

He sentenced Huggins to the minimum allowed, two fifteen-year sentences and a ten-year sentence to be served concurrently.

Huggins has been in prison since Sept. 17, 2014.

"WE DIDN'T KNOW if she was drunk or high that day," Delbert McFadden, one of the twelve jurors who decided Huggins was guilty, told me while describing how he felt about Montgomery's credibility on the stand. I couldn't reach any of the other jurors. They didn't return repeated messages I left.

Fifteenth Circuit solicitor Jimmy Richardson said he's had other cases during which witnesses have recanted. In drug cases, the prosecution is often stuck with less-than-perfect witnesses, he said, and it's not always clear when they are honestly recanting—righting an initial wrong—or doing so out of fear or for another reason.

It happened in an unrelated case seven months after Huggins was convicted. William Christopher Suggs was facing charges for a Leonard Avenue home invasion. His codefendants told the jury Suggs was not involved—even though the prosecution had expected them to say he was.

Suggs was found not guilty.

In the Huggins case, no one was presented during the trial to verify any portion of the statement in which Montgomery named him. How did McFadden and eleven other jurors come to believe the prosecution had proved its case beyond a reasonable doubt?

McFadden did not respond to follow-up queries. He initially spoke to me over the phone, but only briefly. I was only able to ask him how he and other jurors reacted to Montgomery's testimony before he said he was in a rush to get to work and would answer more questions later.

According to the trial transcript, Culbertson speculated the jury must have believed Montgomery's initial statement and disbelieved her courtroom testimony. That would mean the jury believed Montgomery was more trustworthy while being interrogated—when she was sitting in jail trying to avoid a long prison sentence—than when she was under oath, knowing lying could potentially increase a ten-year-sentence she was already serving. That would mean jurors were doing precisely what Culbertson said they could, believe all or none of a witness's statements or testimony.

According to legal experts, direct evidence, like a drug buy caught on video, isn't necessarily more important than indirect evidence. It's up to the jury to decide what passes the "reasonable" test. It means that the American criminal justice system believes it was perfectly reasonable to send Huggins to prison for fifteen years based solely on the word of a crack-addicted woman who admitted lying to protect herself, and perfectly reasonable for a lead investigator to say he lied to solve a crime.

It means it was okay for the lead detective and the prosecutor to tell the jury there was no evidence of

Montgomery's crack addiction—even though there was. It means the system says it is perfectly reasonable to find a man guilty based upon a statement the jury did not even get to fully examine. They were not told Montgomery initially denied everything and that her story included multiple claims that contradict those made by the man police said was the real target of the home invasion.

The verdict was appealed. One such appeal was denied when Richardson argued that Huggins should not get a new trial. This was after Richardson told me that given the paucity of evidence and the unresolved questions, he wouldn't stand in the way of Huggins's attempt to free himself, but that he needed a reason to give to the court. That's the route he would take if Huggins passed a new polygraph test, Richardson said. Huggins "failed" the test again.

Culbertson was the judge who oversaw that appeal, in which Huggins's new lawyer presented new evidence: Montgomery had finally revealed the name of her real coconspirator. She swore to it in an affidavit. Richardson argued it shouldn't be considered new evidence, and Culbertson agreed. Why? Because, the judge said, the defense had an opportunity to uncover such information during the original trial. It's one of the most hypocritical judgments I have ever heard uttered in a courtroom.

During that original trial, only Culbertson had the power to compel Montgomery to reveal that information. He did not use it. He could have held her in contempt until she talked. He could have paused the trial and forced the prosecution and police to examine that new claim, to make sure her testimony was truthful. He could have also forced the prosecution to provide evidence that Montgomery's testimony was affected by threats to her life, as Elder had claimed during closing. He could have done a number of things to ensure that the Huggins trial was fair, none of which he did. He knew what she said was the most important piece of evidence—because there was literally no other evidence. And he knew that because of the nature of the criminal justice system in which he played a vital role, once a conviction occurred, the burden of proof shifts to the convicted, which is why most appeals are denied.

The judge who refused to do everything in his power to ensure the testimony of the star witness was truthful and complete used that incomplete information to deny Huggins a new trial, even after that star witness provided more information and the prosecutor twice used inadmissible polygraph results in a case—just not inside the courtroom—that led to a man being sent to prison based on the word of a crack-addicted woman who recanted on the stand. And everything they did was legal, and you could find legal experts throughout the country who would declare they did nothing improper. I spoke with high-profile judges in South Carolina about the facts of the case. All they could muster was "it's an unfortunate situation" but that the judges and prosecutors made arguments that made legal sense.

In other words, legalese. Heads Huggins loses, tails he remains in prison anyway. His kids lose as well. While

Huggins was being sent to prison based on no evidence, his two young kids struggled to keep up their grades in school, and they struggled at home. They are among the ripple effects those in the justice system rarely consider. It is true that Mariah Eckler's life has been forever altered because of what happened to her and her mom. She did not deserve that. She did nothing wrong. She was the victim. But the same can be said of Huggins's children. They are victims, too, victimized by a system more concerned with technical procedures and practices that can pass legal muster than the well-being of kids who find themselves on the wrong side of the justice system through no fault of their own.

Since his conviction, Huggins has been experiencing the worst of all legal worlds in the U.S. "justice" system. The reasonable doubt standard no longer applies (though it never provided him with justice anyway). He has to find a way to prove his innocence, a nearly impossible standard given the circumstances and nature of his case. Hundreds of men have been freed over the past couple of decades after new evidence was discovered or key witnesses recanted. In this case, the key witness already recanted and there is no new evidence to be discovered—because there was no real evidence presented during the original trial.

There was another factor at play that many lawyers I spoke to said they hardly ever deal with directly—race—despite a growing body of evidence that it is a major factor in jury decision-making, even if unintentional.

Race began playing a role in the Huggins trial from the beginning.

A young black woman walked up to Culbertson and begged out of the jury pool. There's "too much street in this case," she told the judge while visibly shaking.

Culbertson granted her request, allowing one of only a few potential black jurors to leave the jury pool, a jury pool that is mostly white for every criminal trial in Horry County because of other laws and customs governing how a group of potential jurors is culled. That decision, coupled with the philosophy of the Fifteenth Circuit Solicitor's Office to put together a jury based in part on race, all but guaranteed the jury would be homogeneous.

"I don't think race plays as much of a factor in it; I think it's age," Richardson, who heads up the prosecution office in Horry County, told me. "We are all a product of what we grew up in or around."

Multiple studies, such as one by the Equal Justice Initiative that examined juror selection in eight Southern states, including South Carolina, and an examination of Louisiana's Caddo Parish, have shown that most jury pools are overwhelmingly white, and that the relatively few potential black jurors are dismissed at a much higher rate than potential white jurors. The disparate treatment of blacks throughout the justice system makes them less likely to be eligible to vote, which affects their eligibility to be considered for a jury. That reality shows up time and time again in the courthouse where Huggins was convicted.

A growing body of research also shows that the racial makeup of a jury can have an effect on the verdict, even though the Supreme Court in 1986 outlawed the practice of striking potential jurors based on race, a practice critics say still occurs because it is easy for prosecutors to give non-race-based reasons. Richardson freely admits he "would not sit a black male that looks [Huggins's] age" but would allow an older black man because "he might be harder on the young black guy." He makes similar decisions involving white defendants, he told me.

You read that right. The lead prosecutor of one of the largest counties in Trumpland openly says he uses race to decide which jurors to pick and which ones to avoid, and he bases it on racial stereotypes like the one about older black men supposedly being "harder on the young black guy" and the young black guy being too sympathetic to men like themselves. It's the kind of philosophy that is diametrically opposed to the idea of being judged by one's peers. But, like the reasonable doubt standard, in a legal sense *peers* isn't clearly defined, either.

Researchers have found that race has a profound effect on the criminal justice system. "A 2004 study by the Capital Jury Project found that in cases with a black defendant and a white victim, having one or more black male jurors drastically lowered the chances of a death sentence," Gilad Edelman wrote for *The New Yorker*.

Huggins is black and the Ecklers are white; the jury consisted of eleven white people and one black man.

A Duke University study found that black defendants were "significantly more likely than whites to be convicted of at least one crime when there were no potential black jurors in the jury pool." "These findings imply that the application of justice is highly uneven and raise obvious concerns about the fairness of trials in jurisdictions with a small proportion of blacks in the jury pool," the authors wrote.

Still, there's no way to know with certainty how race will affect a particular case, or if it influenced the Huggins trial. But reporting revealed that had McFadden, the lone black juror, been replaced by the alternate juror, Mark Brooks, Huggins would likely be free today.

"I was surprised by the verdict," Brooks told me. "I just didn't find that the witness was credible. I thought there was a lack of evidence. I think [Huggins] may do stuff, but nothing proved he did *that*."

THIS CASE HAS HAUNTED ME for years. I can't stop thinking about it. I've never felt more helpless. If ever there was a set of circumstances that should have forced those in positions of power to reconsider, this is it. And yet none of it matters. The judge got to keep sitting on the bench and sending others to prison. The main prosecutor was able to move into a new job. The lead detective kept his badge and kept doing his job, being paid by taxpayers. The current prosecutor can still rest assured that he is a reasonable and good man who simply wants justice for those harmed in his district, that he is a God-fearing Christian in good standing.

Huggins, though, remains in prison. Outside of his family—who have spent thousands of dollars they can't afford hiring lawyers to try to get him out and holding rallies and protests—no one here seems to give a damn. That's why it has angered me every time I've heard a pundit, political analyst, or Trump apologist tell us all the reasons we should empathize with the supposedly forgotten, economically distressed Trump voter, because they don't give a damn about men like Huggins either.

Now for the Excuses

SHORTLY AFTER U.S. Representative Steve King of Iowa spoke fondly of the term *white supremacy* during an interview with the *New York Times* in early 2019, I contacted a DC-area reporter who had described King's comments as "racially tinged" rather than "racist." He wasn't the only one who used such euphemisms, which had become so common-place in everyday reporting on race that the Associated Press decided to update its stylebook to give reporters better guidance on when it was appropriate to just say "racist" or "racism." I asked that reporter to explain why he went with "racially tinged." He wouldn't speak on the record, but said this: "I have been trained from the begin-ning, as a mainstream journalist, to avoid using words like *lie* and *racist* because they are so severe and it's hard to know, for sure, intent and what's in someone's head."

He personally believes King is a racist, but "my job is not let that infuse my writing," he said. "That doesn't mean I don't struggle with this or am completely comfortable with it or think that the conventions I operate under are adequate to these situations, which include issues of not just racism but lying politicians. One way I deal with this, at times, is to drop the typical descriptors and just let the comments speak for themselves. My goal is to be accurate and fair and get the context right."

It's not the first time mainstream, "objective" journalists struggled with how to report on large groups of white people choosing candidates who openly espoused racism, bigotry, and white supremacy. Of course, during the civil rights era, news outlets throughout the country led by white journalists often ignored the racist terrorism being inflicted upon black people, or even cheered or excused the actions of the domestic terrorists. Though that wouldn't happen in America today, something subtler and more sinister is at play. It was on display in 1990 Louisiana, a precursor to the excuses white journalists, pundits, and analysts deployed to explain away the decision of millions of white people to make a man like Donald Trump president.

The *Atlantic*'s Adam Serwer wrote about how the media tried to explain away why David Duke won almost half the vote in Louisiana and nearly became a U.S. senator because so many white voters chose him. As he summarized:

> Was it economic anxiety? *The Washington Post* reported that the state had "a large working class that has suffered through a long recession." Was it a blow against the state's hated political establishment? An editorial from United

Press International explained, "Louisianans showed the nation by voting for Duke that they were mad as hell and not going to take it any more." Was it anti-Washington rage? A Loyola University pollster argued, "There were the voters who liked Duke, those who hated J. Bennett Johnston, and those who just wanted to send a message to Washington." What message would those voters have been trying to send by putting a Klansman into office? "There's definitely a message bigger than Louisiana here," Susan Howell, then the director of the Survey Research Center at the University of New Orleans, told the *Los Angeles Times*. "There is a tremendous amount of anger and frustration among working-class whites, particularly where there is an economic downturn. These people feel left out; they feel government is not responsive to them."

Think about that. In one instance, even when a politician literally spoke fondly of the term *white supremacy*, some journalists had a hard time labeling the comments as white supremacist. That was particularly odd, given Representative King's disturbing racial history, making it less likely it was just a slip of the tongue. In another, journalists could not bring themselves to grapple with the reality of white supremacy even as a large number of white people tried to make one of the most well-known white supremacists in U.S. history a senator three and a half decades after the Civil Rights Act became law. No wonder the journalistic default was "economic angst" even as Trump rose to national political prominence primarily because of his advocacy for a bigoted birtherism conspiracy theory.

Chris Cillizza of CNN spoke for a lot of white mainstream journalists when he crafted these two tweets days after Trump won the 2016 election. "The assumption that 'Trump voter = racist' is deeply corrosive to democracy. Also, wrong." And: "There is nothing more maddening—and counterproductive—to me than saying that Trump's 59 million votes were all racist. Ridiculous."

He also tweeted this, with a link to a *Washington Post* article: "Donald Trump got Reagan-like support from union households."

So let's start there, with unions and race. According to Philip Bump, the author of that *Washington Post* article, "Trump probably did *better* than Reagan with that core group of white union members."

Cillizza uses that as evidence that it wasn't about racism, given that union members tend to vote Democratic. Others have used such numbers to suggest it was about "economic angst," and that fewer white people would have flocked to an open bigot like Trump if only they had not been struggling financially. Hogwash. It suggests that during the best of economic times for white people, they would have prioritized antiracism and equality. But here in Trumpland, we know that's not true. It wasn't true in the roaring fifties. It wasn't true when the white middle class was being built and expanded by government programs—the G.I. Bill, the New Deal, and housing policies—that were specifically being denied to black people here. It wasn't true when places like the former Georgetown Steel was humming along, employing about 1,400 people at its peak in a small rural county just down from the resort mecca that is Myrtle Beach, South Carolina. During those years, illiterate white men were given jobs overseeing educated black men. In some instances, black men had to do the reading and writing for their white managers to prevent men from being maimed and killed by dangerous equipment. And black nurses' unions in the Charleston area had to protest relentlessly against racial discrimination.

For the *Washington Post* in December 2017, Calvin Schermerhorn, a professor of history in Arizona State University's School of Historical, Philosophical and Religious Studies, detailed how white union workers have repeatedly chosen white supremacy over labor solidarity since after the Civil War.

"As a result of civil rights victories in the 1960s, a Democratic Party coalition of Southern segregationists and Northern unionists cracked apart. Since the New Deal, Democrats had allied with Southern segregationists who tolerated unions so long as they were not in the South. Black civil rights were, in a profound sense, purchased at the expense of a strong and inclusive labor movement," he wrote. "Democrats lost the white South as Republicans appealed to white workers as whites rather than as workers."

Trump's relative success with that group was an extension of effective racist appeals that date back to before Trump came down that golden escalator in 2015.

It was neither an anomaly nor evidence of a nonracist reason to vote Trump. And let us not forget that black workers have been hurt by the shuttering of manufacturing plants just as much as white workers, or more. Trump was unable to convince those working-class Americans to vote for him—because for them, Trump's racism was a deal breaker, no matter what he said about NAFTA.

That's only one of many issues used to excuse the decision to choose Trump. Here in Trumpland, you will frequently hear Trump voters claim they don't oppose legal immigration and are only against people who "violate our laws and sovereignty." But when Trump kicked off his campaign dehumanizing Mexican immigrants as rapists and criminals, Trump voters here defended him, saying drugs are smuggled across our southern border, or "I wish he wouldn't say it that way, but he has a point."

When he called African countries and Haiti "shitholes," they began calling those countries shitholes. When he made it official U.S. policy to steal brown children to dissuade their parents from even seeking asylum—thousands of children who may never be returned—they blamed the brown people fleeing violence and seeking refuge here. When his policies and rhetoric led to a 70 percent drop in legal immigration in one year, they shrugged, even after spending years proclaiming that they were okay with legal immigrants and were only concerned with illegal entry. When Stephen Miller, his primary adviser on immigration, was found to have repeatedly grounded his thinking and research in white supremacist Web sites, it didn't even register with the white Trump supporters I know. They simply didn't care. And none of their jobs or livelihoods were being threatened by undocumented workers, given that where we live, the population is getting whiter.

You'd hear them brag about the state of the economy, with its low unemployment rate—the record-low black jobless rate was a favorite talking point—a long string of monthly job creation, and a stock market that kept breaking records. But during the second term of Barack Obama, when the unemployment rate was falling even faster (the black rate was cut by more than half under Obama), more jobs were being created every month, the stock market was growing more rapidly, and GDP experienced multiple quarters of 4 and 5 percent growth, which has yet to happen under Trump, they parroted Trump and said those numbers were fake. Or they said those numbers didn't matter because there were still empty storefronts on Main Street in Myrtle Beach. They didn't seem to care that their 401(k) values were skyrocketing under Obama, who had inherited the worst economic downturn since the Great Depression. They couldn't seem to stop talking about their 401(k)s because Trump is in office—even as economic inequality was at its highest levels in a century. And after the coronavirus led to Depression-like economic conditions, in part because of the Trump administration's horrifically ham-fisted response, they blamed the virus for their economic struggles and said Trump wasn't being praised enough for the great job he was doing.

It was the same with the nation's deficit. It was a non-stop topic of discussion here beginning with Obama's election in November 2008. I reported on several well-attended, passionate Tea Party rallies during which Trump-voters-in-waiting described the nation's fiscal health as an impending apocalypse. And it was all Obama's fault. That's why they opposed him, not because of race, they made sure to repeatedly tell me. Never mind that under Obama, the nation's deficit was cut by about two-thirds—and under Trump it was well on its way to rising back above the $1 trillion mark before the pandemic made it even worse.

Americans of all races in Trumpland struggle with rising health care costs. It's one thing that unites us like little else. Obama risked his reelection chances to make sure the Affordable Care Act became a reality. That law, while imperfect, has improved or saved the lives of millions of Americans, including many white Trump voters in Trumpland—even former coal miners suffering from black lung. Trump spent much of his first years in office trying to undo that law, without a viable replacement, even as a greater number of poor and middle-class white Americans began suffering "deaths of despair."

Trumpland is often described as among the most patriotic places in the country, largely because of our sizable contingent of military members, retired and active. Respect for our troops is supposedly a Republican strong point and one of the reasons working-class white Americans are loyal to the GOP. But when Trump repeatedly trashed veterans, including Senator John McCain and a Muslim Gold Star family, among many others, Trump voters here did the same two-step they've done while excusing Trump on other issues, either quickly coming up with reasons to claim he was right or offering another half-hearted "Well, I wish he wouldn't do that, but I still support him."

They did the same with morality and strength. They were stalwarts of so-called family values, decency, and civility, and scolded Democrats for not ridding themselves of Bill Clinton. They just don't care about all the immoral things Trump has done and continues doing.

When Obama gave the order to kill Osama bin Laden as his war on terror was leading to the deaths of tens of thousands of terrorists and rolling back most of the territory claimed by ISIS during his term, they said the credit must go to the soldiers, not Obama. When Trump claimed ISIS had been destroyed, they said it was because we finally had a decisive leader in the White House. When Obama used his final year in office to pardon or commute the sentences of more people than all of his predecessors, Trump-voters-in-waiting screamed that Obama was unleashing criminals on our communities. When Trump signed a criminal justice reform bill he likely did not even understand, they cried foul when black people didn't praise Trump as the Second Coming.

That's why black people here knew claims by national political pundits and others that Trump had won because he had spoken to the fears and legitimate concerns of the white working class were largely wrong, or at best incomplete. They had a dozen and a half Republican candidates to choose from before they had to choose between Trump and Hillary Clinton. Enough of them chose Trump during the primaries to make Trump the Republican presidential nominee. Enough of them chose Trump that November to make him president. And they are the only reason he didn't have to mature while in office, as some pundits foolishly believed he would. Trump voter apologists have come up with every reason imaginable to explain away White America's decision to put Trump in the White House—as long as that reason has nothing to do with race. But every time they've had a chance to choose, they've chosen Trump, and continue to. It's time to stop making excuses for their decision to repeatedly support blatant and open racism.

And the biggest excuse of them all has been abortion.

It's also the excuse used to explain away why white Evangelical Christians remained in Trump's corner despite all his ugliness and bigotry since he was elected. *Real* Christians, they are quick to assert, must be pro-life and anti-abortion. *Real* Christians, they declare with righteous anger, must never align themselves with those who are pro-choice, or, in their parlance, "pro-abortion." As a newspaper columnist in Trumpland, I received countless messages from white Evangelical Christian readers declaring that a *real* Christian could not be a Democrat because of abortion. I had the honor of being invited to a two-hour-long presentation detailing why my Christianity wasn't authentic because I didn't pledge allegiance to the so-called pro-life cause. I've had to listen to countless pious white Evangelical Christians tell me why "liberal" Christians are either morally blind or just too stupid to know how immoral we really are. Our refusal to believe that the government should control a woman and her pregnant body for the forty-week gestation period makes us complicit in evil, they've told me. The acceptance of abortion today is akin to the acceptance of slavery in the 1700s and 1800s, they are convinced, which is why Education Secretary Betsy DeVos felt comfortable making the comparison during a speech at a dinner sponsored by Colorado Christian College at the Museum of the Bible in early 2020.

Trump spent much of his life declaring he was "pro-choice in every respect," as he told Tim Russert in 1999. He even said he would not ban "partial-birth abortion," a particular (and misleading) hobbyhorse for those who call themselves pro-life.

"We believe in the right of freedom of speech, freedom of worship, freedom of religion. And we believe in right to life," Trump said while reading from a teleprompter in early 2020 before a crowd of mostly white Evangelical Christian supporters. They cheered.

They were quick to accept Trump's politically convenient change of heart. Even Never Trumpers could not bring themselves to fully oppose Trump because of their views on abortion. They believe that since *Roe* v. *Wade* made abortion a constitutionally protected right, the United States has been involved in a slow-motion genocide that has claimed the lives of several million "unborn" Americans, and that no issue is more import-ant. Trump's bigotry might make them uncomfortable, but Never Trumpers, like Trump supporters, have been buoyed by his appointment of conservative judges. Sup-port of abortion is an absolute red line for them and must be opposed no matter the circumstances. Support of open bigotry and racism is not.

That's the story they tell themselves. The truer one is that there is no evidence—none—that having a pro-life president in the White House has done much to curb abortion. The abortion rate fell more quickly during the Clinton era than under Reagan. The same thing hap-pened when that decades-long trend slowly continued during the two Bush administrations, then accelerated under pro-choice Obama. It fell to a then all-time low under Obama, in large part because of pro-choice policies that prioritized providing comprehensive health care cov-erage to as many Americans as possible over a push for an abortion ban. Also, there is not a significant differ-ence in the abortion rate in countries where it has been outlawed and where it remains legal; it's just that the primary methods of abortion are different where it is out-lawed—and that women having abortions are at a greater risk of harm or death.

If the goal really is fewer, or no, abortions, then wider access to comprehensive contraception, livable wages to help stabilize the nuclear family, closing the achievement and wage gaps between men and women, and a laserlike focus on improving the physical and mental health of women and girls would be more effective than passing laws that might expose women who suffer miscarriages to criminal investigation.

White Evangelical Christians could have used those facts to resist the urge to support Trump. They should have known that even if they had to "suffer" another four years of a pro-choice president to prioritize defeating Trump's open bigotry and racism, the abortion rate likely would have continued falling under Clinton. Though they scream "abortion," they really just wanted Trump. How do I know? Because though they have a Supreme Court majority that could lead to the overturning of *Roe*, they are still sticking with Trump.

They want Trump. They've repeatedly shown us that they want Trump. And they want Trump no matter how many of their previous positions they have to abandon, no matter how much political and moral hypocrisy they have to commit, no matter how much damage he does to brown and black communities.

CNN's Cillizza claims that "the assumption that 'Trump voter = racist' is deeply corrosive to democracy."

I say that not all Trump's supporters are racist, but that they decided to make a racist man president of a rapidly diversifying nation anyway is the greater threat.

I Wish He Didn't,
But Trump Still Matters

THERE'S THE DYED BLOND HAIR down her neck clinging to her shoulders. There's the tight red dress topped with an open short-sleeved leather jacket. There's a black holster around her waist, a black pistol at the ready. She exits a black Ford 4x4 Super Duty pickup truck in the middle of the desert to tell us her name is Michelle Fiore and that she is vying to become Nevada's next governor.

Donald Trump is not in the ad because Donald Trump doesn't have to be. Donald Trump *is* the ad. A TAKE AMERICA BACK Trump 2024 bumper sticker is the first thing you see after the truck comes to a screeching halt. Fiore tells us she spent her whole life "fighting the establishment" the way Trump spent the 2016 election cycle telling us he wanted to fight the establishment. She tells us that she was one of the "first electeds" to endorse Donald J. Trump and "you better believe I was attacked for it," just as Trump repeatedly told us that he was repeatedly attacked for doing what's right.

Fiore crows about being labeled "a gun-totin' calendar girl" by the *Washington Post* and "The Lady Trump" by *Politico.*

"And I don't care," she gloats, though she clearly cares. And a lot.

She isn't the same old compromised boring moderate in a blue blazer like Mitt Romney, whose image is on a cathode-ray tube TV she knocks over in a huff. While describing her "Three Shot" plan, she unholsters the pistol and shoots a beer bottle labeled "vaccine mandates," another labeled "CRT" (critical race theory), and a third labeled "voter fraud."

She closes by telling us "The Joe Biden administration is coming after me," without telling us how or why or when or providing even an out-of-context headline to drive home the point. Because the point is she doesn't have to provide evidence. Being Lady Trump is enough. She's a fighter, remember?

The Fiore ad isn't a Fiore ad. Not really. It's a Donald Trump ad, the latest evidence of his having taken over a major political party that he remains the head of after a humiliating defeat. The ad, released in October 2021, is a reminder that Trump remains all too relevant in this country's politics, psyches, and social debates. Irrelevant candidates like Fiore pledge allegiance to Trump. So do Republicans like Kevin McCarthy, who is hoping to become the next Speaker of the House, and newly elected Virginia governor Glenn Youngkin, who adopted Trumpism even while refusing to stump with him during the campaign.

It doesn't matter that Trump lost the popular vote to Biden by more than seven million, doesn't matter that he is alone among modern-era presidents who saw his party lose the House, Senate, and White House within a four-year span. It doesn't matter that he's a whining man-child stripped of his once powerful Twitter account and has been relegated to ungrammatical, incoherent rantings he releases under the label "Statement by Donald J. Trump 45th President of the United States."

The Fiore ad is a microcosm of what's going on inside one of the two major political parties in the United States of America. The party remains loyal to a man who is loyal only to himself and continues to proclaim the lie that he duly won the 2020 presidential election. The bulk of the party has had its worst instincts unleashed by Trump. This is why previous flirtations with antidemocratic tendencies are now in full bloom among Republicans, and why no matter how conservative your credentials, defy Trump and you will be shunned by the party. Ask U.S. Representative Liz Cheney.

More than nine months after the attempted insurrection and as the Fiore ad was gaining national attention for its gaudiness, Trump released this statement: "The insurrection took place on November 3, Election Day. January 6 was the Protest!"

That's why a little-known gubernatorial candidate in Nevada could make national headlines by clinging to Trump as tightly as Trump clung to that American flag in a now-infamously creepy photo. That's why Republicans you think would know better—who were, briefly, disturbed by the events of January 6, 2021—no longer seem to understand that whatever Trump says goes. That's why we can't turn the page on him, though I desperately wish we would and could.

I, like most Americans, breathed a sigh of relief in November 2020 when Trump was defeated. I don't know how I would have survived another four years of that man in the White House, don't know if the country could have either. But what happened that first Tuesday in November and on January 20, 2021, were necessary steps back toward sanity for the United States, though far from sufficient. Trump was the 2020 loser. That doesn't mean his grip upon one of our two major political parties, and therefore the country, has loosened. His grip on the GOP has only tightened since his loss. As of this writing, Trump is the favorite to win the 2024 Republican presidential nomination if he decides to run or could all but anoint his successor as nominee if he decides not to run.

That's despite his being among the primary causes his party lost full control of Congress and the White House on his watch. That's despite his being caught trying to use taxpayer dollars to bribe another country to launch a politically motivated criminal investigation against Joe Biden, the 2020 Democratic nominee. That's despite the numerous well-detailed crimes in the Mueller report; his inhumane policy of kidnapping brown children at our Southern border; his ignoring the poor and working-class white voters who made him president to prioritize massive tax cuts for fellow ultra-wealthy Americans; dozens of allegations of sexual misconduct; his attempt to make a promised Muslim ban a reality; his casual-transactional racism; his buffoonery; his role in sparking an insurrection attempt.

Trump made a once-in-a-century pandemic worse, his selfishness, his egomania, his callousness likely costing the lives of tens of thousands of Americans. On live TV, the man urged Americans to consider injecting themselves with disinfectant! And yet after it all, about 74 million Americans tried to give him a second term in office, and since then most of them have refused to acknowledge Biden as the legitimate president, while supporting policies and politicians in a variety of states being positioned to overturn the 2024 election if it doesn't go Trump's way again. They have also been busy tightening voter restrictions to increase the likelihood that a Republican like Trump can win the White House largely based on a mostly white share of the vote, ensuring that minority-white rule will remain a real possibility in the United States for the foreseeable future.

I wish none of that was true. I wish I never had to type the name Donald J. Trump ever again in my life, wish you never had to read or hear it. I wish there was a way to rewind time not to 2016 but November 2008, when the nation was electing its first black president. How I long to have another chance to better explain to the unaware that the conditions were ripe for a man like Trump to come along and take advantage of white Americans' fear of a browning nation unlike the one their grandfathers grew up in. I would have screamed louder, would have shouted or cussed or fussed incessantly, whatever it would have taken to awaken those who refused to see the seeds being planted nearly a decade before 2016.

But I can't go back. We can't go back. That doesn't mean we can't take the lessons learned from the past decade and a half and apply them between now and when this country might emerge as a so-called majority-minority nation. That's why this book, unfortunately, remains relevant, more relevant than when it was published in hardcover. Because too many smart people have convinced themselves that the threat represented by Trump is overblown and maybe always was. Because too many usually astute people are so busy trying to protect Trump voters from the label "racist" they have begun to whitewash what he did in office and what a return to office would mean. Because too many people remain focused on spitting matches they've been having with ideological opponents for years, if not decades, instead of grappling with potential dangers that lie ahead.

This isn't a pleasant topic, no time for I-told-you-so's. It remains a hair-on-fire moment even if too many Very Serious People try to convince you otherwise. Trump didn't cause the problems we have. He alone is not responsible for them. That's why his becoming the 2020 loser isn't, unfortunately, the end of the story, though how I wish it were.

When I was writing this book during the final year of the Trump presidency, my hope was that the frank, clear-eyed truth would activate our highest angels and remind us of our highest ideals. That hope remains.

Acknowledgments

Elizabeth Bailey McDaniel gave me life and a voice. While there are countless people for whom I am eternally grateful for helping me along my journey—including my beautiful, brilliant wife, Dr. Tracy Lashawn Swinton, creator of the literacy nonprofit Freedom Readers—that gratefulness begins with my mother. She spoke for me until I could find my voice, all the while making it clear that I would eventually have to speak for myself, no matter how difficult that would be. I'll never forget.

Credits

Chapter epigraph on page 43 from a speech given by Toni Morrison on May 30, 1975 at Portland State University as part of the Public Dialogue on the American Dream series.

A portion of the author's work on the Jamar Huggins case [pp. 113–156] was carried out as part of *Reasonable Doubt*, a six-part special report for the *Sun News*, published September 16, 2015, beginning with "Does the 'beyond a reasonable doubt' standard help or hinder the pursuit of justice?" and "Day 2: Winding, contradictory tale told by crack-addicted witness."

Some of the author's comments in this book previously appeared in "George Floyd, Ahmaud Arbery, and One Journalist's Painfully Honest Self-Examination on Racism," *Nieman Storyboard*, May 29, 2020.

Articles cited in this book include: "Immigration Population Growth in the U.S. Slows to a Trickle," Sabrina Tavernise, *New York Times*, September 26, 2019; "Police Work Isn't as Dangerous as You May Think," Blake Fleetwood, *Huffington Post*, December 6, 2017; "Black Demagogues and Pseudo-Scholars," Henry Louis Gates Jr., *New York Times*, July 20, 1992; "Before Trump, Steve King Set the Agenda for the Wall and Anti-immigrant Politics," Michael Safyan, *New York Times*, January 10, 2019; "Racial divides have been holding American workers back for more than a century," Calvin Schermerhorn, *Washington Post*, December 15, 2017; and "The Nationalist's Delusion," Adam Serwer, *The Atlantic*, November 20, 2017.

ISSAC J. BAILEY is an award-winning journalist and the James K. Batten Professor of Communication Studies at Davidson College. He has been published in the *New York Times*, *Washington Post*, *Charlotte Observer*, *Politico Magazine*, *TIME*, *The Guardian*, and many more, and has appeared on NPR, CNN, and MSNBC. Bailey was a Nieman Fellow at Harvard University and has taught journalism and applied ethics at Coastal Carolina University. He currently lives in Myrtle Beach with his wife and two children.